Steichen at War

Steichen

at War

by Christopher Phillips

Portland House · New York

This 1987 edition is published by Portland House, a division of dilithium Press, Inc., distributed by Crown Publishers, Inc., 225 Park Avenue South, New York, New York 10003, by arrangement with Harry N. Abrams, Inc.

Printed and bound in the United States of America

Library of Congress Cataloging-in-Publication Data

Steichen at war.

  Bibliography: p.
  Includes index.
  1. World War, 1939-1945—Aerial operations, American—Pictorial works. 2. World War, 1939-1945—Naval operations, American—Pictorial works. 3. United States. Navy—Aviation—Pictorial works. 4. Aircraft carriers—United States—History—Pictorial works. I. Steichen, Edward, 1879-1973. II. Phillips, Christopher. III. United States. Naval Aviation Photographic Unit.
D790.S88   1987   940.54′4973   87-10347
ISBN 0-517-63227-6

h g f e d c b a

Project Director: Robert Morton
Editor: Lory Frankel
Designer: Bob McKee

On the title page: Comdr. Edward Steichen photographing from the USS *Lexington.* November or December 1943. *Victor Jorgensen*

Below: Grumman TBF Avenger torpedo-bombers in formation over Fort Lauderdale, Florida. January 1943. *Horace Bristol*

Contents

Preface

During the past half century, more than five million photographs have found their way into the remarkable collection gathered in Washington, D.C., by the National Archives. Since the 1840s, the photographer has been a ubiquitous feature of the American scene, and the images preserved here offer an astonishing overview of the turbulent, kaleidoscopic patterns of American life. Originating for the most part as by-products of the work of government, they have survived not, primarily, by virtue of any aesthetic distinction—although such distinction is not entirely absent. Rather, they have been selected for the unequaled prospect they open onto the American past. The faces and battlegrounds of the Civil War, recorded by Mathew Brady and his collaborators, recall moments of high national drama. Humbler yet equally compelling images unfold in rich detail the vanished forms of the everyday life of the past. Such photographs provide a vivid supplement to the historian's traditional methods, and amply reward the scrutiny of the informed eye.

While the landmarks of this great repository—such as the Brady collection—have long been charted, other of its holdings, less prominent or less easily accessible, contain no less interest. The photographs presented here have been drawn from the more than fifteen thousand prints that make up the original picture file of Edward Steichen's Naval Aviation Photographic Unit. Organized not long after Pearl Harbor by one of the legendary figures in American photography, this small group accomplished a unique visual chronicle of the U.S. Navy during the Second World War.

The relative obscurity of the Steichen unit is surprising, but not difficult to explain. When the photographs were transferred to the National Archives two decades ago, they were separated and redistributed among a half million other Navy photographs from the same period. Today, it requires considerable patience to follow the thread of the Steichen unit's work as it weaves through this much larger fabric. Nonetheless, the effort is rewarding. With the aid of written records, and with the invaluable assistance of several of the group's surviving members, the details of a fascinating photographic enterprise have come to light.

Introduction

Kate Steichen remembers a winter day in early 1942 when one of her fellow employees at a Manhattan department store came rushing over to her. Something in the way she was told, "Miss Steichen! Your *father*'s here!" alerted her that something unusual was in the air. Since the previous December, when the Japanese had attacked Pearl Harbor, her father had been trying, despite his sixty-two years, to find a place for himself in the nation's military. Now she met him coming down the stairway, his gray hair set off by the unexpected deep blue of a Navy greatcoat. At the sight of the uniform, she burst into tears. Her father, Lt. Commander Edward Steichen, quickly enfolded her in a long embrace.

It seems that the Navy's initial puzzlement about what to do with its eager recruit had less to do with his age than with finding the proper use for his talents. Before the war, the Navy's concern with photography was largely restricted to its use as a reconnaissance tool and a training aid. Steichen argued that photography could also serve as an invaluable means to convey the human drama of the Navy's war to the American public, as well as to future generations. The Navy listened, and was, at first, decidedly skeptical.

Convincing skeptics, however, was Steichen's lifelong stock in trade. He possessed, as few photographers have, an appreciation and enthusiasm for the medium's whole range of possibility. His own success at repeatedly reinventing himself as a photographer sprang from this understanding—and from his great natural talents, restless energy, and outsized ambitions. Although he was officially retired when the war began, he saw that it offered the opportunity for another of the self-administered "kicks in the pants" that he recommended every photographer give himself periodically in order to shake off the cobwebs of habit.

Steichen courted change, in part because he was attuned to the ever-changing rhythms of modern life. His work reflected the spirit animating his times. During his long career in photography, he moved confidently through what amounted to several distinct worlds, without ever seeming to drop a beat.

He was born in Luxembourg in 1879, and brought to America by his parents three years later. When his father's health collapsed, from working in the copper mines of Michigan, the family moved on to Menominee Falls, just north of Milwaukee. There his mother encouraged the artistically precocious boy, and it was her indomitable devotion that fixed in him an unflickering self-confidence. He took up photography at fifteen, using it as an aid in preparing commercial illustrations. But for him the camera became more than a predictable means to a mundane end. When, at the age of twenty-one, he set out for Paris, he had already begun to receive serious consideration within the small circle of American photographers who were intently expanding the medium's expressive side.

At its worst, this turn-of-the-century "pictorial" photography clung haplessly to the most hackneyed sentiments of nineteenth-century painting and to a soft-focus technique lifted from Impressionism. At its best, in the work of Alfred Stieglitz, it pointed to the ultimately more rewarding notion that photography could develop its own expressive means—from within itself rather than from painting. En route to Paris, Steichen stopped in New York to pay his respects to Stieglitz; he made—and kept—a promise never to abandon photography.

The first two decades of the new century saw Steichen shuttling between the Old World and the New, dividing his time between Paris and New York, and his creative energy between painting and photography. A photographic self-portrait of 1901 takes pains to certify his image as a painter: wrapped in a dark cape, he brandishes with assurance the signs of his occupation, a brush and palette. But his continuing association with Stieglitz helped give rise to a vigorous American school of art-photography, the Photo-Secession. Its journal, *Camera Work*, and its gallery at 291 Fifth Avenue showed American photographers what could be learned from modern European art. From Paris,

Self-portrait with brush and palette. 1901. *Edward Steichen*. (Reproduced from *Camera Work*, April 1903. Courtesy George Eastman House.)

Steichen sent back what was to be America's first glimpse of the controversial work of Cézanne, Rodin, Matisse, and Picasso.

Steichen's photographs, especially his portraits of the well-to-do, often supported his painting. But in addition to providing a slim income, his blossoming talent as a portraitist led him to seek out the leading artists and writers of the day to sit before his camera. In these portraits he created a soft twilight world, and around them still lingers more than a trace of the rarefied aesthetic air that once circulated in Paris, London, and New York, and that Steichen breathed effortlessly.

That way of life ended abruptly in 1914. As German troops drew near, Steichen, his wife Clara, and their two daughters fled their little farmhouse on the outskirts of Paris. They crossed safely to New York, but three years later Steichen returned to France as a volunteer in the American Expeditionary Force. He was then thirty-eight years old.

That war revealed in him a surprising aptitude for large-scale organization and command. He helped set up the first photographic reconnaissance division for the Signal Corps, and dispatched biplanes twice a day to fly over the trench lines. The typical photograph that resulted might appear to be a crazy-quilt pattern of lines and dots, but a skilled photo interpreter could extract invaluable military information from it. Steichen learned to prize in a new way the camera's ability to render minute detail with utter clarity, and joked that anyone turning in a fuzzy photograph would be court-martialed. When the fighting came to an end on November 11, 1918, Steichen's division remained in France to complete a historical project, a photographic record of the major American camps and battlegrounds.

He came out of the war with the rank of lieutenant colonel and the red ribbon of the French Legion of Honor, which decorated his lapel for many years. The war had swept away the world he had known, and in its melancholy aftermath he experienced a rare moment of disequilibrium. After a period of hesitation,

Major Edward Steichen walks with Gen. M. M. Patrick, Chief of the AEF Air Service, France, 1918.

Steichen redirected his life decisively: he renounced painting, and set ablaze a number of his remaining canvases. He rededicated himself exclusively to photography, but not to the art-photography of an irretrievable past. Steichen spent a year in what he called his second apprenticeship in photography, seeking a new clarity of vision and a new economy of form, bringing every particular of technique within his control. The story is told of his photographing a white cup and saucer against a black background, including a graduated gray scale for comparison of tonal values, for three months, exposing one thousand plates in an effort to obtain complete mastery over his materials. He went on to explore the new language of abstract form, and learned how it might provide a framework to support a realistic vision of the world.

During these years, Steichen resided mainly in Europe. In 1923, at a time when every boat out of New York Harbor carried a contingent of young expatriates who, out of tune with America's postwar boom, were determined to join Hemingway, Dos Passos, and Fitzgerald in Paris, Steichen returned to America to stay. The one-time stalwart of the Photo-Secession shocked his old colleagues by agreeing to photograph for Condé Nast's glossy magazines *Vogue* and *Vanity Fair*, and by signing a lucrative contract to produce advertising photographs for the J. Walter Thompson agency. His turnabout drew raking criticism from Stieglitz and his followers, who loudly bemoaned what they considered Steichen's surrender to material ambition.

Steichen, of course, saw it differently. He wanted his work to carry him beyond the confines of a cloistered elite, toward the center of the pulsating public life of his age. He intended, however, to carry his standards with him. Not unlike his European contemporaries at the Bauhaus, he likened himself to a skilled engineer cooperating with modern industry.

If my technique, imagination, and vision is any good I ought to be able to put the best values of my non-commercial and experimental photographs into a pair of shoes, a tube of tooth paste ... or any object I want to light up and make humanly interesting in an advertising photograph.[1]

Self-portrait, originally published in *Vogue*, October 12, 1929. *Edward Steichen*. (Copyright © 1929, renewed 1957, by The Condé Nast Publications Inc.)

Remarkably, he lived up to his promise, emerging as one of the pivotal figures in the great revolution that overtook magazine photography in the twenties and thirties. These years found him at the height of his powers, seemingly in perpetual motion. For *Vanity Fair*, each week, he photographed the leading personalities of the era; Garbo, Chaplin, Mencken, and Dietrich came to sit before his camera. He said, "I know what light does to things—light dramatizes," and placed his sitters in dramatic, angular spaces created entirely by the slashing beams of studio lights. Crouching before the lens of his big 8 x 10-inch studio camera, wooing and cajoling his subjects, he expertly guided them through a series of moods, gestures, and expressions. For *Vogue*, each week, he photographed the latest fashions; his pared-down compositions dominated the field, and gave rise to a host of imitators.

For four days a week he worked strenuous hours. Then he retired to his Umpawaug Farm near West Redding, Connecticut, to cultivate his acres of prize-winning delphiniums.

The photographic world changed rapidly in the 1930s. Although Steichen's work continued to hold the rapt attention of a wide audience, a younger generation of photographers had sprung up, imbued with the virtues of the unadorned documentary style. They found Steichen's glistening, studio-bound illusions sadly out of date; Walker Evans, one of the more acerbic of their number, claimed to find in Steichen's pictures a "hardness and superficiality" that served as an unsettling counterpoint to the Depression life outside the studio walls.

Although by the late thirties Steichen was an institution, as celebrated as his sitters, he judged that a note of complacency had crept into his work. In January 1938 he abruptly announced his retirement and, after fifteen years, closed up his New York studio. A farewell banquet was thrown at the Algonquin Hotel; it was attended by a host of the leading figures of New York's commercial photography scene, including Paul Outerbridge, Jr., Nickolas Muray, Arnold Genthe, and Anton and Martin Bruehl.

Time remarked, "If Chrysler were to retire from the auto industry, or Metro-Goldwyn-Mayer from the cinema, the event would be more surprising but no more interesting to either business than Steichen's was to his." Noting the austere documentary style that prevailed among younger talents like Berenice Abbott and Walker Evans, *Time* hinted that Steichen's dramatic studio manner belonged to a passing era. It assumed—erroneously—that the exhaustion of a style also signaled the exhaustion of the photographer.

If he found more time to devote to his delphiniums at Umpawaug Farm, even in retirement Steichen never completely cut his ties to the commercial world. During the next four years he found time to take on twenty-five assignments for various magazines. A workable studio and darkroom were constructed in Connecticut, and one of his former studio technicians was engaged as a full-time assistant. He remained one of photography's most outspoken public figures. In 1939 he commemorated the birth of the medium by restoring one of Louis Daguerre's cameras, and using it to produce a self-portrait which beamed out of the pages of *Life* the following week. He kept a sharp eye on contemporary work, serving as an enthusiastic, opinionated picture judge for *U.S. Camera Annual*, an eclectic roundup of the "year's best" published by Thomas J. Maloney, one of Steichen's admirers.

But the ceremonial duties of an elder statesman were not enough. Although nearing sixty, he considered himself not retired, but simply getting his second wind. Occupied more with the future than the past, he entertained visions of grand new photographic projects.

The idea for one such project arose from his deepening concern about America's place in an increasingly threatening world. In 1938, German troops were preparing to march once again in Europe, and Japanese sabers were being unsheathed in Asia. The dismal international prospects, following upon the demoralizing social disruption of the early Depression years, persuaded many Americans of the need to revive the nation's spirit. Steichen was a product of both the Old World and the New, and his commitment to the American ideal was all the stronger for having been freely chosen. His feelings were intensified by his warm admiration for his brother-in-law Carl Sandburg, the poet and biographer of Lincoln. When Steichen came to visit, the two often exchanged ideas during long walks through the cornfields of the American heartland around Elmhurst, Illinois. They came to think of themselves as brothers-in-law who had grown to be brothers. In his long poem *The People, Yes*, Sandburg had expressed an almost mystical faith in the American land and people; in lumbering lines of verse he raised the American "common man" to heroic stature. Steichen had read the poem with enthusiasm, and gradually a parallel project suggested itself to him: a photographic portrayal of the "face of America," in giant photomurals spreading out the riches of its land and people. Wayne Miller (who met Steichen several years later) has recalled:

He told me that before the war, in the late thirties, he had the idea of doing a big show on America—the spirit of America, the face of America, and so forth. He hoped to use the Grand Central Station, paper the inside of that with America, where all the people going back and forth from work could see it, in the heart of Manhattan.

Although the idea never came to fruition, it suggests the heroic scale of enterprise to which Steichen's imagination almost automatically lent itself. And in turning, in his mind, from the studio-bound photography of his past toward the larger world outside the studio, he prepared himself for a vivid encounter with the work of one group of photographers who had already been studying an unsuspected "face" of America.

In the spring of 1938, thousands of New Yorkers lined up for the opening of the International Photographic Exposition. Organized by Willard Morgan (husband of the photographer Barbara Morgan), it was by far the largest display of photographs that the city had ever seen under one roof. Over three thousand images were laid out, the most controversial of which were those submitted by the historical section of the government's Farm Security Administration. These harrowing glimpses of the Depression's human toll, by photographers such as Dorothea Lange, Walker Evans, Arthur Rothstein, and Russell Lee, created a small tempest. Roy Stryker, chief of the FSA's photographic team, wrote to a friend not long after: "It is not exaggerating a bit to say that we scooped the show. Even Steichen went to the show in a perfunctory mood and got a surprise when he ran into our section."[2]

Steichen's enthusiasm for the FSA work was indeed both immediate and abiding. Later that year, he introduced a number of the photographs to the readers of *U.S. Camera Annual*, hailing them as a "series of the most remarkable human documents that were ever rendered in pictures." He emphasized the historical importance of the

FSA's large picture file, which would show later generations the face of America in a critical period. He delighted in the visual and emotional power of the individual images, of "such simple and blunt directness that they made many a citizen wince."[3]

This lesson in the peculiar immediacy of documentary photography was not lost on Steichen. He returned to the FSA work in late 1941, when he began to organize a patriotic exhibition for the Museum of Modern Art. On the eve of America's entry into the conflict raging around the globe, and just before his own formation of a special photographic group for the U.S. Navy, Steichen had the opportunity to examine at first-hand the FSA's operations and accomplishments.

By the fall of 1941, Steichen had come to share Carl Sandburg's presentiment that a "hurricane of fate" lay just ahead, and he was determined to play a role in the national drama that was un-folding. Already, a year earlier, he had attempted to revive his World War I Army commission with the help of his old friend Eugene Meyer, then pub-lisher of the *Washington Post*. But Meyer's support was not enough; in October 1940 he wrote Steichen: "If you want to get into the service, I think you had better come down here and get to work on it yourself. I cannot do it for you."[4] In person, Steichen enjoyed no better success. The Army flatly refused to consider the sixty-one-year-old photog-rapher for active duty.

Thus, in September 1941, Steichen all the more eagerly accepted the proposal of David McAlpin that he organize for the Museum of Modern Art a large exhibition dramatizing the theme of na-tional defense. McAlpin, the museum trustee who, along with Beaumont Newhall and Ansel Adams, had been instrumental in organizing the Museum of Modern Art's Department of Photography the year before, promised Steichen that he could count on the necessary support.

Given a field of action equal to his vision, Steichen's energy was unflagging. Here was the opportunity to realize, at least in part, his "portrait of America." In October 1941 he began an exhaustive search for the images that would convey his message precisely. In the next few months, he handled over one hundred thousand photographs, examining the picture files of Time-Life, the Associated Press, the Tennessee Valley Authority, the departments of Agriculture and the Interior, the U.S. Army and Navy, and the United States Steel Corporation.

But of the one hundred and fifty photographs finally selected, nearly one-third were chosen from the picture file of the FSA. Roy Stryker's photographic team was still in operation in late 1941, although the scope of its coverage—originally, the dispossessed "lower third" of the population— had widened to include the burgeoning defense factories and America's Midwestern "horn of plenty." Steichen visited the FSA's headquarters in Washington, D.C., examined its vast picture file, and studied its methods of organization. Edwin Rosskam, who at that time was responsible for the picture file, remembers that when Steichen arrived, Roy Stryker was on hand to personally guide him around. Where visitors of Steichen's importance were concerned, Rosskam says, "Stryker bestirred himself." Years later, Steichen acknowledged how important the visit had been in preparing him to organize his own unit for the U.S. Navy.

The exhibition, "Panorama of Defense," was scheduled to reach the public the following spring. But the unexpected Japanese attack on Pearl Harbor on December 7, 1941, transformed the nation from an uneasy onlooker to a full-fledged participant in the worldwide conflagration. In many newsstand magazines that December morning could be found an ironic postscript to Steichen's career as a commercial illustrator: a lush color photograph accompanying an advertisement, for Matson Lines, promising "the most pleasant voyage in all the world" to the Hawaiian Islands.

"Panorama of Defense" became "Road to Victory." Steichen, too, was quickly transformed. When, on May 20, 1942, he arrived for a private dinner in the Museum of Modern Art's penthouse to celebrate the opening of the exhibition, he wore the dark uniform of a Naval lieutenant commander. David

Lt. Comdr. Edward Steichen (right) and his brother-in-law, Carl Sandburg, are shown working with a scale model of the "Road to Victory" exhibition at the Museum of Modern Art. May 1942. (Photograph courtesy of the Museum of Modern Art, New York.)

McAlpin, the evening's host, had made certain that figures from Steichen's past, as well as his present, would be on hand. These included (according to the *New York Times*) his sister Lilian and her husband Carl Sandburg; Roy Stryker of the FSA; the aging publisher Condé Nast; and the seventy-two-year-old Alfred Stieglitz.

While the imaginative installation of "Road to Victory" was the work of Herbert Bayer, an innovative emigré designer, its rousing message and rollicking showmanship bore Steichen's unmistakable stamp. Enormous photomurals in dramatic succession unfurled a panorama of the riches of the American earth and the diversity of its people. Carl Sandburg contributed a stirring text to accompany the images.

It was a new kind of photographic exhibition, in which Steichen orchestrated the work of many photographers around a single theme, attaining a level of visual complexity and emotional power seldom before encountered. Beaumont Newhall, the museum's curator of photography, and Ansel Adams, then vice-chairman of the department, had reservations about the extravaganza; they felt that it undermined their continuing struggle to win the museum's support for photography as a fine-art medium. But their doubts were temporarily silenced by the rush of dazzled spectators, whose numbers exceeded all expectations, and by the torrent of critical acclaim.

"It is the most sensational exhibit of photographs that ever was shown in these parts.... What a country to fight for!" exclaimed the left-wing *Daily Worker*. The usually staid *New York Times* reviewer admitted, "It would not at all surprise me to see people, even people who thought themselves worldly, non-chalant, or hard-boiled, leave this exhibition with brimming eyes." Writing in *Photo Notes*, the critic Elizabeth McCausland, one of the day's most acute observers of photography, summed it up: "If we need to be taught a lesson in unity in these days, we can read it in these faces, which might be our own."

At an hour when American military fortunes were at their lowest ebb, "Road to Victory" served as an emblem of the nation's firm resolve. It signaled, moreover, that American photography, like every aspect of American life, was being mobilized behind the war effort. As such, it served as an appropriate send-off for Steichen, who immediately set out for Washington, D.C., to assume personal command of the small group of photographers he had already begun to assemble for the Navy.

After the Army's earlier rejection, how did Steichen succeed, at sixty-two, in winning a Navy commission? The record is tantalizingly unclear. The most intriguing clues, however, have been provided by John Archer Morton, who, having worked for a period in the theatrical world, was in late 1941 a Navy yeoman assigned to the Navy's air station at Floyd Bennett Field on Long Island. Morton was attached to the cadet-selection board, and was responsible for examining the applications of would-be aviation cadets and officers. One morning, sifting through a pile of folders that had accumulated over several weeks, he noted one in particular, for the letters in the upper right-hand corner spelled out a name he recognized at once. At first, thinking it a joke, he called over another sailor to join him as he opened Edward J. Steichen's application to look at the papers. He remembers what he found:

We saw the Croix de Guerre Belgique, with two stars, first; then the Croix de Guerre de France, both of them on fine parchment and richly ornamented; the extraordinary handwriting of General John J. Pershing in a personal message; and the staggering resume issued to Steichen by the Signal Corps, U.S. Army, detailing what his record had been in World War I....[5]

Morton hurried to his commanding officer and volunteered the opinion that Steichen's talents might be of great service to the Navy, and that prompt action be taken lest he turn to some rival service. Morton's sense of urgency proved infectious. His commander quickly telephoned his superior in Washington, Captain Arthur Radford, for instructions. Radford, at that time head of the

Navy's aviation training program, was unfamiliar with Steichen's name or reputation, but the commotion issuing from Floyd Bennett Field persuaded him to act. He ordered Steichen's papers flown to him at once. While a plane was being prepared, a quick call to the offices of Condé Nast Publications took care of the required character references. By afternoon Steichen's papers were in the hands of a courier en route to Washington's airport, where a car waited to whisk them to the Navy Department.

Steichen never learned what had gone on behind the scenes. When he received a call from Radford (apparently not long after Pearl Harbor, although the date is unclear), he described himself as almost crawling through the telephone wire with eagerness. Radford asked him down to Washington to discuss just what role he might be able to play in the Navy.

So the Navy had got Steichen—without really knowing who he was, or what to do with him!

It was a great stroke of fortune that Steichen found himself in the hands of Captain—soon Admiral—Arthur Radford. The Navy, the most close-knit and tradition-bound of the services, was dominated at the beginning of the war by the advocates of battleship power. The Navy's aviators were considered a radical band; Radford, a forceful advocate of air power, was an outsider, in Navy parlance, a "mustang." Willing to listen to fresh ideas and step outside of Navy tradition to get results, Radford rose quickly in the following years, along with the other "carrier admirals" who helped revolutionize the Navy's fighting tactics. His continued support would prove Steichen's chief asset.

Their first meeting, however, seems to have begun awkwardly on both sides. Although he had undoubtedly been briefed on Steichen's age, Radford showed what Steichen considered a flicker of hesitation when they were introduced. According to Steichen's account, his persuasive powers were fully tested.

How could Steichen's particular skills and breadth of vision best be put to use? The omens were not

Capt. J. J. Clark (left) and Rear Admiral Arthur W. Radford on the bridge of the USS *Yorktown*. October 1943. *Charles Kerlee*

favorable, during those early days of the war, that the Navy would turn over to an outsider the job of covering the Navy's war. The Hollywood filmmaker John Ford had run aground on just that issue. Ford had personally assembled and brought to Washington a motion picture crew, and offered the Navy his services in producing a documentary epic of the Navy at war. The Navy had coolly let the idea wither and drop. While Steichen's inclinations also tended to be epic, the Navy's immediate needs were prosaic. Radford offered a solution that satisfied both of them.

Radford, who was then responsible for recruiting and training the Navy's pilots, knew that a fierce battle for talent was under way between Naval Aviation and the Army Air Corps. He shrewdly guessed that photographs for posters and recruiting leaflets might help the Navy attract its quota of thirty thousand new pilots a year. He proposed that Steichen set up a special photographic unit to operate out of the Training Literature division, which was under his command, to follow the story of Naval Aviation, and, incidentally, produce images that would draw attention to the Navy's air wing.

Steichen, undaunted by the limited scale of the operation, must have sensed the larger opportunities that lay ahead. He accepted a Naval rank—lieutenant commander—that was lower than his World War I Army colonelcy. A special medical waiver (on account of his age) was approved on January 28, 1942, and within days he was commissioned as an officer in the U.S. Naval Reserve. His orders were, first, to complete preparations for "Road to Victory" in New York, then to report to Washington for duty.

At about the same time, a young Navy ensign named Wayne Miller was showing Captain Radford some of his photographic work. Miller had studied banking before turning to photography, "nearly killing my father," he recalls. After spending a year at the Art Center School in Los Angeles (where he was told that his photographic talent was doubtful), he enlisted in the Navy in 1941. Although he was assigned to administrative tasks in the Bureau of Aeronautics, photography remained his ruling passion, and he showed his prints to anyone who expressed interest. He remembers being sent to show them to Radford:

Radford said, "These are interesting. We have a photographer coming in, name of Steichen or Stuchen, something like that. Maybe there's a place for you in what he's putting together. He's in New York now, doing a show for the Museum of Modern Art; if you're ever up in New York, you might drop in and see him."

And I heard this name, and it just sent chills down my back. I called and made an appointment and I met Steichen in Tom Maloney's office; the two of them were working on an issue of U.S. Camera *magazine. I showed Steichen the photographs I was so proud of, and he said, "We'll make arrangements for you to get transferred over to my unit." I was thrilled. So I became the first man in his Navy photographic unit.*

Self-portrait in his quarters aboard the USS *Saratoga*. February 1944.
Wayne Miller

On the USS *Yorktown*, Lt. Charles Kerlee steps down from the wing of a Grumman TBF after photographing the raid on Wake Island. He carries two K-20 aerial cameras. October 6, 1943. *Photographer unidentified*

If Miller's principal recommendation was his enthusiasm, Steichen made certain that the other photographers he selected had more experience behind them. He sent out word through his network of professional contacts in New York and Los Angeles that he was looking for crack photographers and skilled laboratory technicians. He sought out men with a variety of skills, not just photojournalists or documentary photographers. Charles Kerlee, regarded as one of the best young commercial illustrators on the West Coast, was recommended by Tom Maloney. Kerlee remembers his reaction to being asked to go into the Navy with Steichen: "I was delighted, since for years I had been clipping and binding into books any of Steichen's work I could find."

Horace Bristol, on the other hand, boasted impeccable credentials as a photojournalist. He had been among the handful of photographers represented in *Life*'s prototype issue of 1936, and

Lt. Comdr. Horace Bristol on Espiritu Santo. February 1944. *Photographer unidentified*

joined its staff on a full-time basis the following year. It was for *Life* that he accompanied writer John Steinbeck on a journey through California's migrant camps, an assignment from which emerged Steinbeck's *The Grapes of Wrath*. Moving over to *Life*'s sister publication, *Fortune*, to free-lance just before the war began, Bristol heard that Steichen was recruiting photographers. He applied and was accepted. If there had to be a war, he thought, serving with Steichen would be an honor and a privilege.

Charles Fenno Jacobs, originally from Boston, had also worked for *Life* in its early days. *Fortune* assignments carried him around the world, and he worked briefly for the Farm Security Administration on a free-lance basis. Despite his reputation as a cynic and bon vivant, seemingly more concerned with gourmet cooking than with photography, he proved one of the most original photographers in the group; an intuitive visual sense and a genuine curiosity about the people he encountered animated his work.

Kerlee, Bristol, and Jacobs were all in their thirties, all established photographers of some reputation. As such, they stood apart from the two younger men, Wayne Miller and Victor Jorgensen. Jorgensen, who had worked as reporter and photographer for the Portland *Oregonian*, had heard of Steichen's Navy group from an acquaintance, Oregon's Senator Dick Neuberger. "He heard about the Steichen unit and wrote me a letter saying, why don't you apply for it? The draft was breathing down my neck, so I did. And it worked out—it was beautiful."

Two photographers whom Steichen had hoped to entice into joining his unit, W. Eugene Smith (lately of *Life*) and Arthur Rothstein (then working for *Look*), proved unable to pass the Navy physical: Rothstein failed to meet the height requirement, while Smith, ironically, was judged too poor in vision.

Thus the "original six"—Kerlee, Bristol, Miller, Jacobs, Jorgensen, and Dwight Long (whose motion picture unit operated more or less independently of the others)—formed the core of the Naval

Lt. Comdr. Charles Fenno Jacobs with an F-56 camera aboard the USS *Iowa*. December 1944. *Photographer unidentified*

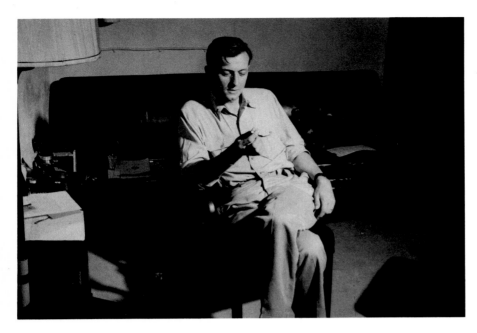

Lt. Victor Jorgensen in the quarters he shared with Comdr. Edward Steichen on the USS *Lexington*. November or December 1943. *Edward Steichen*

Aviation unit until late 1944, when additional photographers were taken on. Steichen admitted, later, that his selections had "caused some eyebrows to be raised." But he insisted that the variety of talents he had assembled ensured that "the final document would, as a result, present not any one point of view, but a balanced pictorial symposium leading to an objectivity not one photographer could obtain."[6] He had also chosen men who would require little training, who could go to work immediately to establish a beachhead of support within the Navy. According to Miller, "Each one of us had our own qualities, but Steichen had assured himself that he had pros. Every one of them was a proven professional except me."

Obtaining a group of first-rate photographers was only the first step for Steichen. He knew the value of expert technical backup, and won permission to set up a separate laboratory facility to serve his unit exclusively. Technicians from around the country were recruited by Leo Pavelle, whom Steichen knew as the owner of one of New York's best commercial laboratories. Situated in the Fisheries Building on Independence Avenue, the unit's lab was lavishly outfitted to the most advanced professional standards.

Lt. Comdr. Dwight Long with a 16mm motion picture camera. March 1945. *Photographer unidentified*

Among the technicians recruited by Pavelle was young Marty Forscher, who was assigned to learn camera repair. Forscher was one of the few technicians to start out as a relative novice—most of New York's professional repairmen at that time were of German origin and thought to be dubious security risks for war work. Forscher's lack of experience was quickly remedied. He remembers that on the first day he reported for duty, he collected samples of all the cameras he might encounter. He disassembled the first one piece by piece, shuffled the pieces in a box, and proceeded to teach himself how to put it back together again. Then he went through the remaining cameras in the same way. He rapidly became a legend with the unit for his ability to restore reputedly unsalvageable equipment. "Nobody ever had such good care as we did," recalls Horace Bristol.

On June 5, 1942, six of the Navy's air stations around the country were notified that Steichen, Charles Kerlee, and Wayne Miller would shortly begin a rapid tour of the installations. By that time, Steichen and his second wife, Dana, had moved to Washington's Georgetown section for the war's duration. Wayne Miller had already begun to organize an office in the Navy's temporary building on Constitution Avenue, where the Bureau of Aeronautics's Training Literature division was located.

Here were gathered a group of men who before the war had been professional writers and illustrators; now they were engaged in streamlining the Navy's aviation training materials in anticipation of a flood of new enlistees. Steichen's new unit was conceived as the photographic branch of the operation. According to Miller,

Steichen was working really back in his own world; working with professionals when it came to the visual image as well as the written word. Because of his age, presence, and experience, people looked to him, because they recognized in him someone who knew how to make these things work.

Feeling a certain pressure to achieve immediate results, Steichen assumed an active personal role in the first photographic assignments that summer. The most striking images that he and his photographers produced were turned over to the Navy's public relations office, or were used to illustrate recruiting posters. Before long, as the full crew of younger photographers became available, he spent less time traveling and more time attending to administrative chores in Washington. Not the least of these involved defending his unit from sharp attacks from within the Navy. Steichen's name may have carried formidable weight within the relatively circumscribed photographic world, but it counted for much less, at first, among the Navy's admirals. The Navy's own photography school at Pensacola, one of the most highly regarded of those in all the services, was a great source of Navy pride. What was the need for a special photographic unit brought in from outside?

Steichen was determined to bring home to the Navy the lesson that other government agencies had learned in the thirties: that photography, in addition to serving as a simple recorder of facts and faces, could, in the right hands, serve as a powerful instrument for distilling the human meaning of complex events. But until he had demonstrated the value of images that were both strikingly photographic and understandably human, there were several storms to be weathered.

Early on, Steichen had convinced Radford that his photographers should be brought in as officers, to ensure them the freedom of maneuver they would need in order to do their jobs. The Navy's photographic officers traditionally did very little actual picture-taking; instead, they supervised enlisted men who did. If it was considered upsetting that Steichen's men planned to take their own pictures, it was deemed outrageous that they intended to carry their own photographic equipment. The Navy was not accustomed to seeing its officers carrying anything more cumbersome than a pair of white gloves; enlisted men carried the burdens. Thus, when Steichen's photographers set out loaded with cameras and supplies, they met a chilly reaction, and found few helping hands extended. However, with Radford's support, Steichen fought off loud complaints that Navy tradition was being grievously undermined. Victor Jorgensen recalls that there was "always some sort of cataclysmic hoorah going on," and remembers one encounter with the frosty Chief of Naval Operations, Admiral Ernest J. King:

I was trotting down one of those mile-long corridors in the Navy Department on some sort of job, with both hands full of gear, when who comes steaming down the corridor but the King himself—E. Jesus King. What do I do? I can't salute him—I've got my hands full. I should have dropped everything and snapped to attention, but I didn't. I got by him, and one of his coterie peeled off and came alongside. "What's your name? What's your number?" I guess Steichen got read off a little for that one, because that was strictly not done in the Navy. But we got away with it, one way or another.

Carrying their own cameras suggested a maverick streak in Steichen's new unit; the cameras they carried confirmed it. The Speed-Graphic, the Navy's standard-issue camera, was a sturdy machine, but hardly designed for quick operation. The photographers of the Naval Aviation unit liked the smaller, more manageable roll-film cameras like the Rolleiflex, and Steichen, like his European contemporaries, was very interested in introducing the 35mm "miniature camera." The Navy, initially, had no provision for ordering such exotic equipment, but a way was quickly found to skirt the problem. Miller discovered that color film, which was then largely unavailable on the civilian market, could be bartered for the needed equipment and supplies at Washington's camera stores. After that, crates of 8 x 10-inch Kodachrome film (which, Miller recalls, was "worth its weight in gold") began to arrive regularly at the unit's headquarters. Later, when their unorthodox equipment had proved its worth, it became easier to order supplies through Navy channels.

For the first six months of the unit's existence, Steichen kept the Naval Aviation photographers

closely within the bounds of their original mission.
While he told Wayne Miller that their job would
eventually be to photograph the U.S. Navy at war,
for the moment they were kept busy compiling a
visual record of the Navy's air training program.
Flight trainees were followed through their program
of calisthenics, swimming instruction, lessons in
hand-to-hand combat, glider exercises, and on
into flight training. Steichen took the job seriously,
and threw himself into the thick of activity when
he accompanied the younger men on an assignment.
Victor Jorgensen recalls his first encounter with
Steichen:

*When I got to Washington, Steichen and Kerlee were
down in Florida doing some training pictures. He
telephoned up and ordered me down there, so I rattled on
down to Jacksonville. I don't remember what the name
of the hotel was, but there he was, you couldn't miss him.
He was sixty-two, or something like that, but he had
more energy than the rest of us put together. When I got
there, why poor Kerlee had been run right down to the
knees. He ran me ragged. For sixty-two, he had fabulous
energy. He could go eighteen hours a day at dead flat
out—and he'd do it.*

Steichen probably realized that the assignment
for the training division had to be carried out
letter-perfect if his group was to have a chance at
a larger role. And, during the summer of 1942, it
seemed more and more likely that the Navy's air
groups would play a decisive role in the Pacific
theater. The success of the carrier-launched Japanese
attack on Pearl Harbor, which had sent six American
battleships to the bottom, also scuttled the notion
that the battleship was the key to control of the
sea. The naval battles of May and June 1942, in
the Coral Sea and at Midway, failed to produce
the expected confrontation of opposing lines of
heavily armed battlewagons. The surface ships
never even made contact, as squadrons of wide-
ranging, carrier-borne aircraft neatly upset all the
old equations. At Midway, a Japanese force of
eleven battleships retired rather than risk facing
two American aircraft carriers. It took time to
work out the tactical implications of this new kind

The American flag flies over the USS *Santee*.
November 1942. *Horace Bristol*

of naval warfare, but few could deny that the Navy's airmen represented a crucial factor in the struggle ahead.

The photographers of the Naval Aviation unit knew that if they bided their time they would soon have a chance to follow into combat operations the trainees with whom they had spent so much time. Horace Bristol was first. During the summer of 1942 he traveled regularly down to Norfolk, Virginia, to photograph a Naval air squadron there, going aloft with the aircrewmen to capture images of the air formations in flight. That fall, the squadron leader suggested confidentially that Bristol might like to join them on an interesting tour that was coming up. As anyone who read the newspapers could have guessed, an Allied landing in North Africa was about to take place. Bristol quickly got permission to accompany the carrier USS *Santee* when it sortied from Bermuda on October 25, 1942, with other carrier groups, on their way to rendezvous with the Allied armada in mid-ocean.

Bristol's photographs of Operation Torch attracted wide attention at the Navy Department. He showed the convoy spread out across the Atlantic under a dramatic sky, then-novel scenes of life aboard the carriers, and aerial views of the first landings on the Moroccan coast in November. One picture in particular, which simply showed the American flag snapping crisply over the *Santee*'s deck, was reprinted widely; although it was an image of a kind that was later overworked to the point of cliché, for the moment it seemed to sum up the nation's resurgent confidence and fighting spirit.

Bristol's success helped tip the scales, as far as the Navy establishment was concerned. In addition, the somber portraits that Steichen produced, in his old studio style, of Secretary of the Navy Frank Knox, Under Secretary James Forrestal, and Chief of Naval Operations Ernest J. King helped establish personal ties at the highest levels. Navy officers who had previously been hesitant to take a chance on Steichen's outfit now began to come around with ideas. Captain J. J. Clark, a

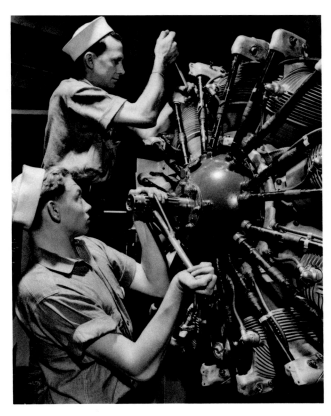

Aviation machinist trainees working on an aircraft engine at Navy Pier, Chicago, Illinois. July 1942. *Photographer unidentified*

friend of Radford's who would prove to be one of the most successful of the carrier skippers, stopped by the Washington office to request that one of Steichen's photographers accompany him on a practice run to New Caledonia. Charles Kerlee was assigned the job, and Clark hit it off well with him. When Clark was ordered back to the United States to take command of a new "fast carrier," the USS *Yorktown*, he added Kerlee to his staff, along with Dwight Long, the unit's motion picture specialist. The *Yorktown* was launched from Norfolk in the spring of 1943, and headed for the Pacific, where the Navy was assembling its newly built ships and freshly trained crews for its first major offensive campaign. Before many months, they would be joined by the other members of Steichen's unit—and by Steichen himself.

Steichen successfully weathered a bureaucratic buffet in March 1943. As his sixty-fourth birthday drew near, he was notified that, having reached retirement age, he was being removed from the active-duty list. Admiral Radford, who had previously served as his first line of defense in such

A Naval air base in the Aleutian Islands during a blizzard. March 1943. *Horace Bristol*

Part of the U.S. fleet anchored at Adak harbor in the Aleutians, preparing to move against the Japanese base on Kiska. The Japanese abandoned the island before the attack could be launched. August 1943. *Horace Bristol*

departmental disputes, was no longer on hand, having recently assumed a carrier command in the Pacific. Steichen launched an immediate appeal to Navy Under Secretary James Forrestal, who promptly sent word that he was to continue his present duties. For good measure, Steichen soon received notice of his promotion to full commander.

By that summer, as the Naval Aviation unit marked the end of its first year of existence, its circle of activity quickly began to expand. Horace Bristol went north to follow the Navy's campaign against the Japanese in the Aleutian Islands off Alaska, and was present for the aftermath of the battle for Attu in May. Wayne Miller accompanied a Navy group to Brazil to inspect the quartz mines that were secretly furnishing crystals for sophisticated communications systems. Fenno Jacobs toured the aircraft factories of both American coasts, suggesting something of the enormous home-front changes wrought by the war in his pictures of young defense workers—many of them women— lunching under the omnipresent camouflage netting.

As their opportunities widened, Steichen encouraged his photographers to propose their own assignments and itineraries; they were in the field more often than he was, and presumably in closer touch with what was going on. Although occasionally Steichen might suggest general topics that he felt ought to be covered at some point, the Naval Aviation unit never developed detailed "shooting scripts" such as those Roy Stryker had furnished to his FSA photographers. More and more, remembers Wayne Miller, "we could just go out and pursue our instincts, with the tremendous responsibility of coming back with something. But he had this faith, he would bet on the individual— and it paid off."

Steichen's real contribution was more subtle, and sprang from his concern with showing the war's impact on the everyday citizen-sailor. While he recognized the need to continue serving up a certain number of pictures that could be useful to the Navy in a publicity sense, his overriding interest lay in photography's ability to make vivid the drama of ordinary men caught up in extraor-

A PBY-5A Catalina patrol bomber searches for signs of enemy activity in the Aleutian Islands. March 1943. *Horace Bristol*

dinary events. Miller remembers him saying, "I don't care what you do, Wayne, but bring back something that will please the brass a little bit, an aircraft carrier or somebody with all the braid; spend the rest of your time photographing the man." Miller recalls, "It was Steichen's prime concern—don't photograph the war, photograph the man, the little guy; the struggle, the heartaches, plus the dreams of this guy. Photograph the sailor."

In October 1943, Charles Kerlee accompanied the *Yorktown*'s pilots on an air strike against Japanese-held Wake Island. The attack was a prelude to the much larger Operation Galvanic set for November, when the Navy's new ships and planes would have to clear the way for the Marines' amphibious assault on Tarawa and Makin, in the Gilbert Islands. Wayne Miller, on November 5, planned to join the USS *Saratoga*'s Air Group 12 on its mission against the heavily defended Japanese stronghold at Rabaul, on New Britain. He relinquished his seat, however, to a ship's photographer who wanted to accompany one air strike before he returned home; the unlucky photographer returned, his body riddled with bullets, his last frame showing a Japanese Zero closing in.

With the Navy about to launch its first major offensive in the South Pacific, Steichen was no longer content just to watch his photographers' pictures flow back to Washington. He contacted Radford, who arranged for him to sign on for temporary duty aboard Radford's former flagship, the USS *Lexington*, accompanied by Victor Jorgensen.

According to Jorgensen, when they arrived in Pearl Harbor in early November 1943 to meet the *Lexington*, Steichen discovered that his reputation had preceded him.

There was a riot before we went on the Lexington. *Of course, Steichen's fame in the Navy was considerable after some of the admirals found out that he'd soaked old man [J. P.] Morgan five thousand dollars for one shot. So we hit Pearl Harbor and all of the admirals wanted to be photographed by Steichen. Okay, Steichen*

Comdr. Edward Steichen perched on the framework below the flight deck of the USS *Lexington*, photographing with a K-20 aerial camera. November or December 1943. *Victor Jorgensen*

says, fine, he'll do it. We set up shop out on Ford Island and had a parade of the whole works of them come by; we worked on that thing about two weeks before we got through with them. But I think we shot every darn one.

Steichen's own best-known photographs of the war resulted from his tour on the *Lexington*, called the "Blue Ghost" because the enemy claimed so often to have sunk it. During the long voyage from Hawaii to the Gilbert Islands, he and Jorgensen roamed freely throughout the ship, photographing the daily routine of the vessel's three-thousand-man crew. Steichen was enthralled by the incredible scene on deck during takeoff and landing operations. On the second day at sea, he was busily photographing the ship's landing signal officers at work. While he was standing with his back to the incoming aircraft, one plane came in unexpectedly fast and low; it skidded across the deck and swept directly over the spot where Steichen would have been standing—if the signal officers had not pulled him along into the safety net below their perch. Jorgensen, who had seen the runaway plane plunge over the side, anxiously ran to see what had happened.

I had dashed down the deck fully expecting to find the Old Man spread all over the platform, but had only gotten about halfway when he and the two LSOs climbed up on the flight deck and sauntered toward the bridge. His second words were:
"I think I got it!"
"Got what?" I asked.
"The picture," he grinned. "Right when the thing was overhead."[7]

As the task group to which the *Lexington* belonged drew near its target, Steichen turned to the anxious scenes that were being played out in the pilots' ready room. The Navy's tactics, drawn up by the battleship admirals, positioned the carriers in defensive sectors to provide close cover for the Marine landing on Tarawa. The airmen argued that this would only attract swarms of Japanese attackers; they wanted to use the carriers' swift striking power to take out the enemy's airstrips before the landings began. Their arguments were overruled. Operation Galvanic proceeded as planned.

Steichen was reluctant to see Jorgensen go aloft with the airmen. "I didn't hire you to get you killed," he said. But on December 4, 1943, the *Lexington* itself came under attack. Early that morning, Admiral Charles A. Pownall ordered planes from the carriers to attack the Japanese airstrips on Kwajalein, in the Marshall Islands, and to bring back reconnaissance photographs of the atoll. At 6:30 A.M. the first planes left the *Lexington*, the *Yorktown*, and the *Cowpens*. A succession of difficulties followed, and faulty intelligence kept many of the pilots from finding their targets. Returning members of the first strike spotted a flock of Japanese long-range torpedo-bombers—called "Bettys"—parked on nearby Roi atoll. The *Yorktown*'s Captain J. J. Clark argued for an immediate strike against them, but Pownall disagreed, and ordered the American ships to retire. On the *Yorktown*, Clark exclaimed, "Goddamit, you can't run away from airplanes with ships!"[8]

He was proved right just before noon, when four Japanese "Kate" torpedo-bombers came in low, avoiding radar, and made straight for the *Lexington*. Three were stopped by the ship's gunners, but the fourth loosed a torpedo that the ship narrowly escaped. Half an hour later, when a second flight of "Kates" headed for the *Yorktown*, Steichen mounted the *Lexington*'s deck with an aerial camera to record the scene. Two of the attacking planes were destroyed by cruiser and destroyer fire; a third turned back. The fourth, however, closed rapidly and was less than 150 yards from the *Yorktown* when its gunners tore off the plane's wing with a 40mm shell. Charles Kerlee and Dwight Long continued to record the action throughout the attack.

The attack was renewed that night, when a full moon in a cloudless sky set the scene for a visit from the "Betty" torpedo-bombers that had earlier been sighted on Roi. Around 8 P.M., enemy "snoopers" began to drop float lights and brilliant parachute flares to guide the "Bettys" in. The full moon made the artificial illumination almost superfluous. For five and a half hours the task force was pursued by circling aircraft, while Pownall sent the ships through desperate (and highly effective) evasive maneuvers.

In a remarkable passage in *The Blue Ghost*, his account of the voyage, Steichen remembers suddenly feeling that the moon, the subject of some of his earliest paintings and photographs, had now turned betrayer. "All hell is let loose around us. . . . How I now hate that smooth bland moon, want to scratch it out, blast it to smithereens."[9]

Around midnight, Victor Jorgensen recalls, "They visited us, and one of their torpedo-bombers dropped an acoustic torpedo. Ours never worked,

A Japanese "Kate" torpedo-bomber is hit by a 40mm shell from the USS *Yorktown*. December 4, 1943. *Chief Photographer's Mate A. N. Cooperman (a ship's photographer on the USS* Yorktown)

but theirs did. It banged us in the number three screw, and blew us into a locked turn. It was only a matter of half an hour until they could get her straightened out, but it seemed like eternity."

Finally, at 1:30 A.M., the moon sank below the horizon and the attack subsided. At sunrise, Steichen rose and found the *Lexington*'s exhausted young sailors, still wearing their helmets, collapsed with fatigue on the ship's deck.

After limping back to Pearl Harbor, the *Lexington* sailed on to Seattle for repairs. Determined to spend Christmas with his family in Connecticut, Steichen reached Grand Central Station as the last train was boarding on Christmas Eve. His daughter Kate remembers him describing how he called out, as the conductors moved to close the doors, "Hold it for the Navy!" and scrambled aboard.

The lessons of Operation Galvanic brought on a crucial rethinking of the Navy's fighting tactics in the Pacific. New "fast carrier" forces were organized to go on the offensive, ranging deep into enemy waters to rain unremitting blows on the Japanese fleet. The carriers now occupied the centers of the fighting formations, ringed by protecting battleships and cruisers, and an outer screen of destroyers. Instead of returning frequently to home ports for resupply, the carrier forces now stayed at sea while a flotilla of oilers, ammunition barges, provision ships, and repair vessels journeyed out to meet them—a logistical performance of incredible sophistication and scale. The Navy's airmen had not only proved their worth, they had helped rewrite the Navy's book on strategy. For the remainder of the war, the prime naval objective for both sides was to "get the carriers."

The new prestige of the carrier forces undoubtedly rubbed off on Steichen's Naval Aviation photographers, who had been with them from the beginning. On the walls of Navy offices around the world, the old reproductions of paintings of sailing vessels came down, and were replaced by dramatic photographs of the carrier-centered task forces of the Pacific.

Lt. Barrett Gallagher in the rear seat of a Curtiss SB2C Helldiver, carrying a K-25 aerial camera. January 1945. *Photographer unidentified*

One of the most important fruits of the unit's growing official recognition was the approval of a system of "open orders," which Radford and Clark helped work out with the Navy's commander-in-chief in the Pacific, Admiral Chester Nimitz. Steichen's men were granted an unprecedented freedom of movement to enable them to cover the vast distances of the Pacific war zone. They could board any ship they wished in order to take photographs, and they could claim priority in arranging air travel from place to place. In Jorgensen's words, "That was something extra—we could go anywhere we wanted, we could stay as long as we wanted, and come home when we wanted."

The sight of official orders instructing the bearer simply to "proceed where you deem necessary" occasionally gave rise to suspicions that the photographers were Navy Department "spies"

Short Chronology of the War in the Pacific

1941 *December 7:* Japanese warplanes attack Pearl Harbor.

1942 *April–May:* American forces surrender in the Philippines.

May: Battle of the Coral Sea.

June: Japanese advance halted at the Battle of Midway.

August: Marines land on Guadalcanal.

1943 *May:* Attu, in the Aleutian Islands, is taken back from the Japanese.

November: First major American naval offensive in the Gilbert and Marshall islands. Marines land on Tarawa.

Map by Paul J. Pugliese

1944 *January–February:* American landings on Majuro, Roi, Namur, Kwajalein, Eniwetok, and Truk islands.

June: Battle of the Philippine Sea.

June–July: Landings on Saipan, Tinian, Guam.

October: Battle of Leyte Gulf. MacArthur's forces land on Leyte.

1945 *January:* MacArthur's forces land on Luzon.

February: Marines land on Iwo Jima.

March: Manila captured.

April: Landings on Okinawa.

August 6: Atomic bomb dropped on Hiroshima.

August 9: Atomic bomb dropped on Nagasaki.

August 14: Announcement of Japanese surrender.

September 2: Surrender ceremony on the USS *Missouri* in Tokyo Bay.

BERING SEA

Attu Adak

ALEUTIAN ISLANDS

ALASKA

PACIFIC OCEAN

50°

40°

30°

20°

Wake

Midway

HAWAIIAN ISLANDS

Kaui Oahu

Pearl Harbor

Honolulu

Maui

Hawaii

ebi Bikini

MARSHALL ISLANDS

wetok Roi

10°

Kwajalein Namur

Majuro

Mili

170°

0°

Makin

Tarawa

GILBERT ISLANDS

180°

170°

160°

150°

SANTA CRUZ ISLANDS

ritu NEW HEBRIDES

sent out from Washington to surreptitiously monitor performance. A more common reaction was simple incredulity. Barrett Gallagher, one of several photographers who joined the unit late in 1944, has written that on his first assignment he requested temporary duty on the staff of Admiral Gerald F. Bogan. "He had not heard of me and he asked me what my orders were. On an Irish impulse I told him my orders were to go anywhere I liked, do whatever I wanted, and go home when I felt like it. After he had read them he said, 'Damned if they don't,' and took me on."

Finally in a position to seriously get on with the job of documenting the Navy's war, Steichen would sometimes hold conferences to suggest special topics that needed to be covered. But he was still more likely to encourage the younger photographers' intuition than to check it. They began to spend more and more time in the field, carrying

Marine Sgt. Paul Dorsey stands beside the wreckage of a Japanese aircraft on Guam. Fall 1944. *Photographer unidentified*

A homeless child in the streets of Naples, Italy. August 1944. *Wayne Miller*

photographic provisions to see them through two and three months at a time. As the Navy and Marines began, in 1944, to climb the long chain of islands that led to Japan's home waters, Steichen obtained the services of Sergeant Paul Dorsey, who had been a news photographer and photo-journalist before enlisting in the Marines, to provide coverage of the Marines' bitter struggle against their determined foe.

The new mobility enjoyed by the Naval Aviation photographers is evident in the circuit traveled by Miller in 1944. The youngest, least experienced member of the original group, he was the most determined to prove himself as a photographer. In 1944, he managed to photograph his way around the world. In February he covered, from the air, the Marine landings on Engebi island. In March he sailed on the USS *Saratoga* to the Indian Ocean for a joint operation with Lord Louis Mountbatten's British fleet. In August he was in the Mediterranean, photographing air operations off the coast of southern France, and stepping ashore at Naples. There, feeling that this, too, was part of the job of photographing the war and its human consequences, he made many photographs of that city's uprooted children wandering the streets in rags and searching for food among the rubble. By the year's end he was back in the South Pacific, on board the USS *Ticonderoga* before its pilots launched the first strikes against Japanese-held Manila. In a letter, Steichen offered him a mixture of assessment and advice:

I think you are turning 'em out of a quality that warms the cockles of the old man's heart. Don't worry about [a well-known photographer]—you are headed in a warmer and more human direction—don't be afraid to move in on close-ups—Shoot more color—that's the only way to get national circulation.... The status of the unit gets better all the time.... Keep 'em coming—I'm betting on you—ready to give you my odds. My best to you and lots of it.[10]

In Washington, Steichen remained largely desk-bound. All of his life he had been the man

A mother and her children in war-damaged Naples, Italy. August 1944. *Wayne Miller*

behind the camera; that job now passed to younger men. But if they served as his surrogate eyes, he was able to bring more than four decades of accumulated visual understanding to bear on the flood of raw imagery that flowed back to his office.

He was an uncompromising perfectionist. He insisted that the photographers under his command return their exposed film to Washington rather than attempt to process it in the field; he knew that careful, controlled processing was the first step toward the picture quality that he demanded. He saw to it that the unit's lab was run along strictly professional lines: all chemicals were regularly tested, all prints and negatives were washed until residual chemical traces had vanished. From the negatives, contact sheets were prepared and sent directly to Steichen's office; there, he and his assistants scrupulously inspected them all. The unit's photographers could request any prints they wished from the laboratory. But it was Steichen who determined which ones would join the unit's active picture file (modeled on that of the FSA), and which would be classed "reserve negatives." Wielding an editor's blue grease pencil, he indicated not only which images were to be enlarged, but how they should be cropped and printed. The print quality he demanded from the laboratory was notoriously high. Work that failed to meet his standards went back to be repeated, often accompanied by the instructions that the lab printers learned to chant in unison: "Deeper, darker, DOWN!"

Marty Forscher, the unit's repair specialist, recalls that whenever Steichen announced a personal inspection of the lab, a nervous buzz would start to circulate there. If a batch of supposedly identical prints was on hand, ready to be sent out, Steichen sometimes liked to conduct an on-the-spot com-parison. Pulling two prints from the top of the stack, two from the middle, and two from the bottom, he would toss them on the floor and scrutinize them intently. Unless they matched up tone for tone, without exception, he would order the whole lot printed over again.

This relentless attention to detail paid off, of course, and handsomely, when the photographs were circulated to the civilian press. John G. Morris, *Life*'s wartime picture editor in London, has emphasized the sense in which the Second World War was the still photographer's war.[11] With the emergence of television as a mass medium yet a decade away, the image of the war that reached most American homes was supplied by the stream of photographs reproduced in the pages of newspapers and magazines. The papers and, especially, the big picture magazines were always eager to provide an inside look at the Navy in action, and Steichen was able to furnish them with the kind of exciting, technically superb photographs that they wished their own photographers had made.

Clearly, Steichen edited for a combination of human interest, graphic power, and an epic sense of spectacle. While he recognized that magazine photojournalism typically weaves a story out of a series of related pictures, he showed a special talent for isolating the single, stunning image that contains the whole story in itself, and halts a viewer in his tracks. Oliver Jensen, a writer for *Life* before the war, and for the Navy after Pearl Harbor, has recounted the enormous relief he felt upon discovering a group of photographers within the Navy who could supply the kind of pictures with which he was accustomed to working. Steichen, by virtue of his understanding of the magazines' picture needs, his wide-ranging personal contacts, and his undeniable flair for promotion, emerged as one of the Navy's most effective wartime communicators.

Ironically, his very success in placing his unit's work before the public—in newspapers like the *New York Times*, magazines like *Life* and *Look*, and books like Jensen's *Carrier War*—contributed to his photographers' chief complaint. The Navy, unlike some of the other services, prohibited individual picture credits; all of its photographs were released under the anonymous legend "Official U.S. Navy Photograph." Despite his efforts, Steichen was never able to have the rule relaxed. His men, who for the most part had been working professionals before the war, thus found themselves at a distinct disadvantage to civilian photojournalists like Robert Capa and W. Eugene Smith, who were at least assured of due credit for the risks they ran. There was occasional grumbling on the part of some of the men that they were risking their lives in the Pacific, while Steichen was reaping all of the glory back in Washington. It was an eerie echo of a similar complaint lodged against Mathew Brady, nearly one hundred years earlier, by the photographers who worked for him during the Civil War.

The men who served under Steichen undoubtedly realized that, in spite of his sixty-five years, his effort was no less than theirs. In late 1944, he wrote to his sister Lilian of putting in long hours seven days a week. "I'm working harder than ever and it is beginning to tell a little. But there is no alternative. The job is growing and it must be done."[12]

By the fall of 1944 Steichen was able to report confidently to Admiral Radford on his group's accomplishments, and to outline his next plans. The original unit was expanded to include additional photographers, including Barrett Gallagher, John Swope, Thomas Binford, and Charles Steinheimer. Steichen hoped to assemble a large illustrated book, *Naval Aviation at War*, with the help of *U.S. Camera*'s Tom Maloney and the backing of the American photographic industry. The motion picture footage that Dwight Long had obtained on the *Yorktown* and other carriers was being turned into a feature-length documentary by Louis de Rochemont, originator of the "March of Time" newsreels, and 20th Century-Fox. And Steichen himself was preparing another spectacular photographic exhibition for the Museum of Modern Art, to open in January 1945.

Dwight Long's film, *The Fighting Lady*, which reflected Steichen's insistence on showing what the war looked like from the average sailor's point of view, proved a great popular success. The home-front audience was probably most impressed

Part of the exhibition "Power in the Pacific" at the Museum of Modern Art. January 1945. *Photographer unidentified*

by the riveting sequences of air combat. Long had loaded color motion picture film into cameras synchronized to the planes' wing guns, and set the cameras to keep running briefly after the guns had ceased firing. The resulting footage seemed to put the viewer into the pilot's seat, to wrenching effect.

The exhibition at the Museum of Modern Art, "Power in the Pacific," also met a warm reception. Meant to sum up the war in the Pacific as seen through the camera's lens and the photographer's eye, it featured Steichen's selections from the work not only of Navy photographers, but of

Capt. Edward Steichen photographing Chamorro children on Guam.
March 1945. *Charles Kerlee*

those from the Marines and Coast Guard as well.
As in the exhibition "Road to Victory" three
years earlier, a loose dramatic narrative was presented through a succession of giant enlargements.
The enlargements were the work of the unit's
Washington lab, which had had to improvise a
method of printing the largest murals. Marty
Forscher remembers that exposures were made a
section at a time, and the prints—some up to
eight feet long—processed on the floor by barefoot
technicians who wielded mops laden with chemicals.

Navy Lieutenant George Kidder Smith, an
architect and photographer before the war, was
assigned to design the exhibition. He remembers
having had "an enormous amount of stimulating
fun" working with Steichen on the project. They
had a sharp disagreement, at one point, over
which photograph should lead off the show.
Steichen (who had been made a captain not long
before, giving rise to the sobriquet that remained

with him for years afterward) was at first insistently in favor of a picture of a battleship firing its big guns. Kidder Smith came up with a photograph (by Fenno Jacobs) of a group of cheering sailors.

With only a small amount of trepidation I said to the Captain that I thought that this would "key" the show better than the firing guns. "Kidder, you are absolutely right," replied the Captain—while two others on the project fell off their chairs. He was that kind of person: brilliant, demanding to the millimeter, contagiously enthusiastic, and always receptive to the ideas of others.

As the war entered its final six months, additional duties came Steichen's way. He was named director of the newly created Naval Photographic Institute, and was made responsible not only for his original unit, but for all of the Navy's combat camera crews. The Institute was charged with developing ways to apply photography as a medium of both historical record and public information—exactly the uses to which he had directed his Naval Aviation unit.

His new duties took him to the Pacific for a second time, in March 1945, to inspect the photographic facilities at the Navy's new Pacific headquarters on Guam. Late that month, just after the Marines had secured the tiny island of Iwo Jima after some of the war's bitterest fighting, Steichen set foot on the island's black beaches. Accompanied by Tom Maloney, now a war correspondent, Steichen saw a "desolate mass of rocks, steel, and tangled vegetation," the burned-out remains of aircraft, and the fragments of the vessels that had carried the Marines ashore. He underscored the human carnage in a photograph of the lifeless fingers of a buried Japanese soldier sticking up through the rubble. In counterpoint, he also showed a small white flower, "the only living thing in sight," hesitantly poking out from amid the debris.

On April 12, 1945, Steichen was back in the United States, visiting a New England shipyard, when the news came over the wire that President Franklin Roosevelt was dead in Warm Springs, Georgia. He quickly called the unit's Washington

Capt. Edward Steichen talks to a Marine corporal on Iwo Jima. March 1945. *Photographer unidentified*

office and urged Fenno Jacobs and Wayne Miller, the only photographers on hand, to try to capture the reaction of the people on the streets of the capital. Miller remembers that he needed no instructions—he was already at work as the newspaper headlines began to trumpet the news, freezing stunned pedestrians in their footsteps. On Saturday morning, April 14, he was waiting at Union Station when the train carrying Roosevelt's casket arrived from Georgia. The casket was placed on a caisson drawn by horses, and its progress was accompanied by muffled drums. As the cortege moved slowly through the streets of the capital, Miller walked beside it, trying somehow to capture on film the emotions he saw etched in the faces he passed. He remembers feeling disembodied, almost invisible, as he walked along, seeing the many hands raised in improvised salutes, and the many faces glistening with tears.

Carl Sandburg wrote to him, not long afterward, speculating on what it might have meant if a similar document could have been made after Lincoln's death. Sandburg told Miller that he found this series of photographs as deeply moving as any he could recall, and assured him that he would return to these photographs again and again.[13]

The end of the war in Europe on May 7, 1945, turned all eyes to the final act of the drama being played out in the Pacific. General Douglas MacArthur had fulfilled his promise and returned to the Philippines, cutting the Japanese off from precious raw materials, and the Navy and Marines had reached the edge of the Japanese home islands. No one was predicting, though, when victory might come. The bloody fighting on Okinawa in April and May was accompanied by the appearance, in force, of Japan's kamikazes, whose suicidal tactics proved dangerously effective against the American warships. The savagery of the fighting and the desperation of the foe convinced American planners that Operation Olympic, the projected fight for a foothold on the Japanese mainland, might cost the full first three waves of soldiers and Marines—one hundred and fifty thousand men. To subdue Japan entirely might require one and one-half million casualties.

In July, Admiral Radford sent word to Wayne Miller, then in Europe, to report at once back to Washington. There, the puzzled Miller was advised to arrange for immediate transportation to Guam. On Guam, he was told to board a Marine troopship about to sail for an unannounced destination. No details were given. When they had been at sea for a short time, word came that on August 6 the Japanese city of Hiroshima had been reduced to cinders by a single atomic bomb; three days later, a similar fate befell Nagasaki. The Japanese sued for peace—on the single condition that Emperor Hirohito retain his throne—and Miller's troopship was ordered on to Tokyo Bay.

During the days of uncertainty after the surrender was announced, when it was not clear if the agreement would survive, Admiral William F. Halsey ordered his Third Fleet to an area several hundred miles southeast of Tokyo, where the ships remained on alert. On August 16 and 17, 1945, as it became apparent that the peace would hold, they were joined by elements of the British Pacific fleet and carried out a series of maneuvers in unusually tight formation—maneuvers staged expressly for the camera. Lieutenant Barrett Gallagher of the Steichen unit flew in a plane overhead, capturing the climactic images of massed American naval power. Operation Snapshot, as it was called, was followed a few days later by Tintype, a companion exercise that saw American warplanes fill the skies. On September 2, Gallagher was one of the many photographers who crowded on board the USS *Missouri* in Tokyo Harbor to witness the final surrender ceremony, bringing to a close more than three and one-half years of fighting.

Wayne Miller had been with the Fourth Marines when they landed to spike the guns of the harbor. After covering the joyous liberation of American prisoners of war held in the Tokyo area, Miller joined up with *Life* photographer J. R. Eyerman and accompanied him to Yokohama,

where they located a Japanese-American friend of
Eyerman's who had been interned since the
beginning of the war. The three decided to set
out for Hiroshima, which had just been opened
to correspondents, and was accessible only by
train.[14]

About September 5, they boarded a train
crowded with Japanese soldiers who had just
been demobilized and ordered home. The
Americans were apprehensive, not knowing quite
what to expect from their fellow passengers so
soon after the end of hostilities. They discovered,
however, that since the Emperor wished the
fighting to cease, his still-loyal subjects would obey.
The Americans found themselves politely ignored,
for the most part, during the twenty-one-hour
journey. As they traveled through central Japan,
they saw, at the way stations they passed, Allied
prisoners of war gathering for the returning train,
which would carry them to Tokyo.

Miller and Eyerman reached Hiroshima on a
gray, drizzly day, and found an almost deserted
city. A lone Japanese soldier in a black cape stood
on the plain created at the blast center. Survivors
huddled in the few buildings that remained
standing, nursing their wounds and blast burns.
Flies swarmed thickly about them. In a Buddhist
temple, the cremation of bodies had already begun,
and the ashes placed in ceremonial boxes tied
with a distinctive ribbon. The man who tended
to them seemed hardly to notice the presence of
the two Americans with cameras.

The euphoria that swept through America at
the war's end prompted all of the services to
rapidly demobilize. Since those who had spent the
most time overseas were the first detached, most
of the members of the Naval Aviation unit were
out of uniform by Thanksgiving. A truck arrived,
one morning, at the unit's Washington laboratory
and began to haul off the photographic equipment
and supplies stockpiled during the war.

Before he left active duty on October 22,
Steichen arranged for a ceremony to honor the
war's outstanding Navy, Marine, and Coast Guard

photographers. His own contribution was recognized on November 6, when he was awarded the Navy's Distinguished Service Medal by James Forrestal, now Secretary of the Navy; the citation commended his "exceptionally meritorious service" in using photography to train the Navy's flyers, to inform the public about the course of the war, and to create an invaluable historical record.

Most of the men who had served under Steichen were able to turn their experience to good advantage. Wayne Miller returned to Chicago, where, with the aid of a Guggenheim award, he began to document the lives of that city's black population. Charles Kerlee returned to advertising photography, in New York rather than Los Angeles, and quickly made a name for himself as one of that city's leading commercial illustrators. When he needed a camera repaired, he took it to Marty Forscher, who had set up shop on Lexington Avenue.

Some found it more difficult to settle down after the years of globe-hopping. Probably the most ambitious scheme was that hatched by Horace Bristol, Victor Jorgensen, and Fenno Jacobs. In December 1945 they marched into *Fortune*'s offices in full uniform, wearing the ribbons they had won in the Navy. As a hedge against finding themselves in competition for the same jobs, they proposed to divide the world into three parts, each to be covered by one of them for a year and a half. *Fortune* enthusiastically agreed to guarantee them enough money to keep going. Bristol, who had dreamed up the three-way plan, took Asia, where he spent the next two decades based in Japan. Jorgensen chose Africa, and Fenno Jacobs headed for Europe.

His job in Washington at an end, Steichen returned home to Connecticut late in 1945. His daughter Kate remembers that for his arrival she had planned a victory celebration complete with laurel wreath. When he finally appeared, however, she quickly realized that dwelling on the war's immense human tragedy had badly deflated his spirits. A celebration was not appropriate. She quietly put the laurel wreath away.

Steichen closed out his involvement with Naval photography in 1946, when he compiled and edited *U.S. Navy War Photographs*, one hundred pictures that summarized the events from Pearl Harbor to Tokyo Bay. The large, blue-jacketed paperback was intended as a memento for the Navy's men as they returned to civilian life, and was brought out by Tom Maloney's US Camera publishing company. Suppliers and printers provided their services at cost, and within six months, Maloney has estimated, nearly six million copies were sold at thirty-five cents each.

At sixty-eight, still too energetic to face retirement, Steichen took charge of the Museum of Modern Art's photography department, in the summer of 1947. At that time he looked back on his recent accomplishments with pride in a job well done. He was certain that his Navy unit's photographs would provide a rich historical legacy for the future; at the war's end, James Forrestal had ordered the "Steichen file" maintained as a separate group.

In the Navy I started with a handful of good photographers who became experts, not only in using a lens but in photographing with their hearts and minds. The influence of that handful spread to 4000 Navy photographers. Not all were great photographers. But they all contributed to the story of the war. And there has never been anything like the photographic story of the last war.[15]

He remained haunted by the war's incalculable toll of human misery. In his autobiography, he tells of his earlier hope that photography, by revealing the true face of war, might help banish its specter. It was one of photography's most enduring, and most illusory, dreams. "Here are the dreadful details," Alexander Gardner had said eighty years before, hoping that his images of the "black horror and reality" of Gettysburg's aftermath might help forestall another such calamity.

In 1948, Steichen told an audience, "During my lifetime our country has had three wars. I have been a photographer in two of them. I don't want to do it again. I want to photograph the light on the countenances of men and women who are at peace."[16] His experience during the war years had convinced him that photography could speak to the great questions of the day with a powerful public voice. In the face of the apocalyptic rhetoric of the Cold War, he urged photographers to make plain the issues that unite, rather than separate, humanity. He felt that in such perilous times, photography's greatest contribution lay in "explaining man to man across the world." From this belief, born of his war years, ultimately sprang the vast exhibition of 1955 that Steichen considered his greatest bequest to the human family—"The Family of Man."

1. Quoted in Carl Sandburg, *Steichen the Photographer* (New York: Harcourt, Brace and Company, 1929), pp. 54–55.

2. Quoted in F. Jack Hurley, *Portrait of a Decade: Roy Stryker and the Development of Documentary Photography in the Thirties* (New York: DaCapo Press, 1977), p. 132.

3. Edward Steichen, "The F.S.A. Photographers," *U.S. Camera Annual* (New York: US Camera Publishing Company, 1939), p. 44.

4. Eugene Meyer to Edward Steichen, October 10, 1940; Meyer correspondence, Library of Congress.

5. John Archer Morton, "How the Navy Got Steichen," unpublished manuscript, 1979.

6. Edward Steichen, "Twelve Great Pictures of the War," *Art News Annual*, December 1944, p. 100.

7. Victor Jorgensen, "Captain, USN," *Infinity*, December/January 1954/1955, p. 9.

8. Quoted in Clark G. Reynolds, *The Fast Carriers* (New York: McGraw-Hill Book Company, 1968), p. 107.

9. Edward Steichen, *The Blue Ghost* (New York: Harcourt, Brace and Company, 1947), p. 125.

10. Edward Steichen to Wayne Miller, undated correspondence, 1944.

11. John G. Morris, "This We Remember," *Harper's*, September 1972, pp. 72–78.

12. Edward Steichen to Lilian Steichen, undated correspondence, fall 1944.

13. Carl Sandburg to Wayne Miller, correspondence, May 15, 1945.

14. See J. R. Eyerman, "The Tokyo Express to Hiroshima," *Life*, October 8, 1945, pp. 27–35.

15. Edward Steichen, quoted in George Bailey, "Photographer's America," *New York Times Sunday Magazine*, August 31, 1947, p. 39.

16. *Utica* (N.Y.) *Observer-Dispatch*, December 11, 1948.

Editor's Note: The pictures are arranged thematically rather than chronologically. The croppings of the prints follow Steichen's original specifications.

Making the Machines of War

For Americans, World War II was a war of mass production, of transport, and of machines. Following Pearl Harbor, President Franklin Roosevelt called upon industry to turn out fifty thousand warplanes each year—a staggering demand. Working around the clock, aircraft plants not only met but surpassed that goal. Shipyards, too, bristled with activity: the Navy, which had entered the war with only six operational aircraft carriers, boasted well over a hundred by August 1945.

Most of the eight million Americans who had been unemployed before the war went either into uniform or into the factories. With so many men in military service, employers were forced to overcome their reluctance to hire women to fill what had previously been considered men's jobs. More than four million women joined the work force during the war years; in the aircraft assembly plants, they accounted for four out of every ten workers. These dedicated "Janes who made the planes" captured the popular imagination, and were celebrated in songs such as "The Lady at Lockheed" and "Rosie the Riveter."

A worker assembles machine-gun turrets at the
Glenn L. Martin aircraft plant in Baltimore.
February 1943. *Fenno Jacobs*

At a 1,700-foot-long assembly line at the Douglas aircraft plant in El Segundo, California, workers prepare the fuselages of dive bombers. August 1943. *Fenno Jacobs*

Construction of PBY seaplanes at the Glenn L. Martin aircraft plant in Baltimore. The fuselages are hoisted on special jigs to be tested for watertightness; the water is placed inside the hull and inspection takes place outside. February 1943. *Fenno Jacobs*

Riveters working on the wing panel of a Douglas SBD Dauntless dive bomber at the Douglas aircraft plant in El Segundo. August 1943. *Fenno Jacobs*

A workman at the Vega aircraft plant in Burbank, California, scrapes smooth a plaster cast
in which plexiglass will be molded to fit a
machine-gun turret. August 1943. *Fenno Jacobs*

Two workmen lay down camouflage netting at the Consolidated Vultee aircraft plant in San Diego, California. August 1943. *Fenno Jacobs*

A shift goes off duty at the Consolidated Vultee
aircraft plant in San Diego. August 1943. *Fenno
Jacobs*

A worker eats lunch at the Consolidated Vultee aircraft plant in San Diego. August 1943. *Fenno Jacobs*

A quartet of workers at the Vega aircraft plant in Burbank during lunchtime. August 1943. *Fenno Jacobs*

Workers at the Consolidated Vultee aircraft plant in San Diego eat lunch sitting against aircraft wing panels. August 1943. *Fenno Jacobs*

Workmen check the wing-operating mechanisms of an F4U Corsair at the Chance-Vought Corporation, Stratford, Connecticut. March 1943. *Photographer unidentified*

Workmen at the Vega aircraft plant in Burbank spin the propeller of a finished airplane. August 1943. *Fenno Jacobs*

Workers inside the Douglas aircraft plant at El Segundo prepare the engines that will power SBD Dauntless dive bombers. August 1943. *Fenno Jacobs*

America Strikes Back

The Japanese offensive that was launched at Pearl Harbor rolled on through Singapore, the Philippines, and Guam before it was stopped at Midway Island in the summer of 1942. The Navy could not mount its own offensive, however, until new warships had been built and new crews had been trained. The Navy's pilot training program expanded from three hundred trainees a year to twenty-five thousand. Before receiving combat assignment, each fledgling pilot was put through twelve to fifteen months of preflight instruction and flight training by veterans who had been rotated home. By the war's end, the Navy had fielded over sixty thousand pilots.

While the Navy's Pacific fleet, crippled at Pearl Harbor, was being rebuilt, there was a war to wage in the Atlantic. In addition to keeping the shipping lanes to Europe open for convoys of matériel, the United States unleashed its first offensive blows. Horace Bristol's photographs of Operation Torch, the Allied assault on North Africa in November 1942, offer early views of the Navy's carriers and their crews at sea. Bristol sailed on the USS *Santee*, an escort carrier whose pilots provided air cover for the American landings at Safi, 150 miles south of Casablanca in Morocco. There, Navy flyers skirmished briefly with French airmen still loyal to the Vichy regime.

Navy pilots waiting in an office of the Naval Air Transport Service in Miami, Florida, prior to their departure on a training flight to Trinidad. August 1943. *Wayne Miller*

Douglas SBD Dauntless dive bombers flying over
the Naval Air Station at Daytona Beach, Florida.
October 1942. *Horace Bristol*

Young Navy aviators file out of the mess hall at
the preflight training school at Del Monte, California. July 1943. *Fenno Jacobs*

Sailors gathered in a hangar at the Banana
River (Florida) Naval Air Station. March 1943.
Edward Steichen

Sailors shipping out from San Diego, California. June 1942. *Photographer unidentified*

A Grumman TBF Avenger torpedo-bomber being hoisted aboard the USS *Santee* at Norfolk, Virginia, before joining the Allied fleet to take part in Operation Torch. October 1942. *Horace Bristol*

Enlisted men going through their exercises on board the USS *Santee*, en route to Africa to take part in Operation Torch, the Allied landings in Morocco. November 1942. *Horace Bristol*

Part of the two-thousand-vessel Allied convoy crosses the Atlantic during Operation Torch, bound for the North African coast. November 1942. *Horace Bristol*

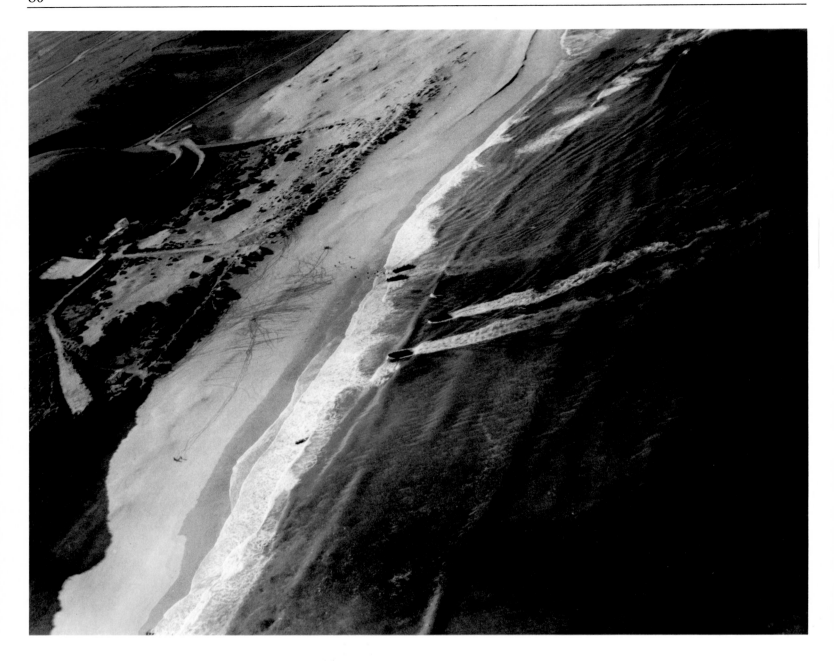

Above: Operation Torch: aerial view of the first landing on North Africa. November 1942. *Horace Bristol*

Left: Lt. Comdr. J. T. Blackburn, after spending sixty-four hours in the Atlantic waiting for rescue, is hoisted from a tanker to the USS *Santee.* November 1942. *Horace Bristol*

Right: A carrier silhouetted against the Atlantic horizon, en route to North Africa to take part in the Operation Torch landings in Morocco. November 1942. *Horace Bristol*

Convoy Life – Meeting the Enemy

During the long weeks it took for an assembled Naval task force to get under way and to cross the vast stretches of the Pacific, the ships' crewmen alternated between combat drills and more relaxed off-duty activities, such as playing cards, writing letters, and reading. Each man was assigned a general quarters station; he was expected to rush to it when the general quarters alarm signaled that contact with the enemy was imminent.

Air reconnaissance, radio communication, and radar were essential to coordinating offensive and defensive maneuvers. With the advent of air power, sea battles might take place over areas covering several hundred square miles. As it became clear that the carriers held the key to naval power, the flattops were placed at the center of defensive battle formations. Attacking Japanese dive bombers or torpedo-bombers, searching out the carriers, could expect to face spirited opposition: first, from squadrons of defensive fighters; then, from the concentrated artillery fire of the destroyers and cruisers ringing the carriers; next, from the fighters of the combat air patrol, which circled high above the carriers; and, finally, from the blazing fire of the carriers' own gunners.

Fast-carrier Task Force 58 in the South Pacific.
1944. *Photographer unidentified*

Enlisted men relaxing on the USS *New Jersey*
during off-duty hours. December 1944.
Fenno Jacobs

Enlisted men exercise on the deck of the USS
Yorktown. October 1943. *Charles Kerlee*

Navy crewmen transferring a torpedo from a
submarine tender to a submarine about to leave
on patrol. May 1945. *Horace Bristol*

A U.S. submarine on war patrol in the Pacific. July 1945. *Horace Bristol*

Lt. Comdr. John R. Madison prepares to go up the ladder from the control room of the USS *Muskallunge*, at the submarine base at New London, Connecticut. August 1943. *Edward Steichen*

Ordnancemen of the USS *New Jersey* moving a 16-inch shell from its stall to an ammunition hoist. November 1944. *Fenno Jacobs*

A gunner on the battleship USS *New Jersey* lowers the breechblock in preparation for loading the shell into a 16-inch gun. November 1944. *Fenno Jacobs*

Gunners of the USS *New Jersey* packing in the
bags of powder that will fire the shell of the
16-inch gun. November 1944. *Fenno Jacobs*

The USS *Missouri*'s 16-inch guns fire six projectiles. November 1944. *Photographer unidentified*

A sailor asleep between two 40mm guns on the battleship USS *New Jersey*. December 1944. *Fenno Jacobs*

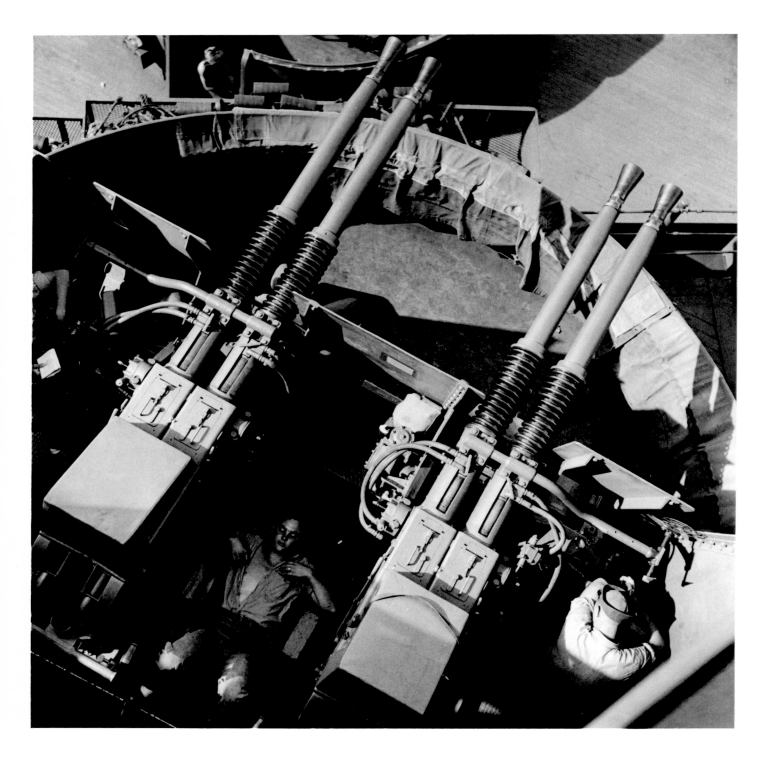

The forward stack of the USS *New Jersey*, en route to the Philippines. December 1944. *Horace Bristol*

Vice Admiral John S. McCain (left) confers with Admiral William F. Halsey on board the USS *New Jersey*, en route to the Philippines. December 1944. *Fenno Jacobs*

A Marine gun captain on the USS *Lexington* points out a Japanese "Kate" torpedo-bomber moving in to launch a torpedo. December 1944. *Edward Steichen*

On the USS *Hornet*, 20mm-gun crews stand by at their stations as planes from the carrier fly to Tokyo on a bombing mission. February 1945.
Charles Kerlee

A burning Japanese torpedo-bomber falls after
being knocked down by artillery from American
warships. December 4, 1943. *Edward Steichen*

Crewmen of the USS *Yorktown* dash across the deck to their stations as the signal for general quarters sounds. May 1943. *Charles Kerlee*

Gunners of the USS *New Jersey* watch flames rising from the carrier USS *Intrepid* after it was struck by a kamikaze off the Philippines. November 25, 1944. *Fenno Jacobs*

Firefighters of the USS *Intrepid* battling blazes caused by a kamikaze hit during the battle for Leyte Gulf. November 25, 1944. *Barrett Gallagher*

Sailors sleeping on the flight deck of the USS *Lexington*. November 1943. *Edward Steichen*

Enlisted men, exhausted after more than twenty-four hours at general quarters, sleep on the deck of the USS *Lexington*. December 5, 1943. *Edward Steichen*

Burial at sea for the officers and men of the USS *Intrepid* who lost their lives during the battle for Leyte Gulf in the Philippines. November 26, 1944. *Barrett Gallagher*

Carrier Life – Launching the Attack

An aircraft carrier is a noble thing. It lacks almost everything that seems to denote nobility, yet deep nobility is there. A carrier has no poise. It has no grace. It is top-heavy and lop-sided. It has the line of a well-fed cow. . . . Yet a carrier is a ferocious thing, and out of its heritage of action has grown its nobility. I believe that every Navy in the world has as its No. 1 priority the destruction of enemy carriers. That's a precarious honor, but a proud one.

Ernie Pyle, Last Chapter, *1945*

The 3,000-man crew of a heavy carrier like the USS *Yorktown* existed to support an air group of 175 officer-pilots and 130 enlisted gunners and radiomen. Naval airmen were charged with a variety of missions, including patrol and photoreconnaissance duties, attacks on enemy airstrips and naval installations, air support of amphibious operations, and bombing raids against the Japanese fleet.

A carrier's complement of 100 fighters, dive bombers, and torpedo-bombers was maintained on a cavernous hangar deck within the ship, and was brought up to the flight deck by elevators. Before a mission, the airmen of each squadron would gather in a ready room off the flight deck to review flight instructions and weather data. As the flattop turned into the wind in preparation for launching its planes, specialized crews of plane handlers, signal officers, and fire fighters went into action amid the whirling propellers on the flight deck. One by one, the planes were sent aloft, where they joined in formation and headed off for their target.

Infrared view of officers gathered on the deck of the USS *Lexington*. November 1943. *Edward Steichen*

The flight deck of the USS *Saratoga* at dawn, as the ship moves in for an air strike against Rabaul. November 1943. *Wayne Miller*

Aerial view of the USS *Cowpens*. July 1945. *Barrett Gallagher*

The air plot room of the USS *Lexington:* fighter director Lt. Comdr. A. F. Fleming (with pipe) and radarmen direct combat air patrols during a strike in the Marshall and Gilbert islands. November 1943. *Edward Steichen*

Pilots of the USS *Lexington* in the carrier's ready room on the eve of the air strike against Kwajalein. December 4, 1943. *Edward Steichen*

Aircrewmen of the USS *Ticonderoga* in the ready
room, preparing for the first air strike against
Manila. November 5, 1944. *Wayne Miller*

A torpedo ready to be loaded onto a Grumman
Avenger torpedo-bomber on the USS *Suwannee*
in the South Pacific. January 1943. *Charles Kerlee*

Navy crewmen bringing up a Grumman F6F
Hellcat fighter by elevator to the flight deck of
the USS *Monterey*. June 1944. *Victor Jorgensen*

A plane handler on the USS *Saratoga* guides a Hellcat into position for the trip down the elevator and onto the hangar deck. November 1943. *Wayne Miller*

Crewmen hastily drag a plane with a flat tire down the flight deck of the USS *Lexington* to make way for another plane to land. November 1943. *Edward Steichen*

Pilots of the USS *Hornet* rushing to their planes
for a mission in the China Sea. February 1945.
Charles Kerlee

Aircrewmen of the USS *Saratoga*'s Air Squadron 12 walk to their planes before carrying out a raid on Rabaul (left to right: Ens. Charles Miller, Lt. Henry Dearing, Lt. Bus Alber). November 5, 1943. *Wayne Miller*

A Navy pilot hurries to his torpedo-bomber on the USS *Monterey* to take part in a strike against Guam. July 1944. *Victor Jorgensen*

Grumman TBF Avengers take off from the
flight deck of the USS *Monterey* for a mission
over Tinian. June 1944. *Victor Jorgensen*

The pilot of a Grumman F6F Hellcat awaits the
takeoff signal on the USS *Lexington*. December
1943. *Edward Steichen*

A Grumman F6F Hellcat rolls down the deck of
the USS *Lexington* for takeoff. November 1943.
Edward Steichen

A Grumman F6F Hellcat takes off from the
deck of the USS *Lexington*. November 1943.
Edward Steichen

A Grumman F6F Hellcat takes off from the
deck of the USS *Lexington* during operations
in the Marshall and Gilbert islands. November
1943. *Edward Steichen*

Aftermath of Battle

Landing operations provided some of the most hazardous moments of carrier life, especially if returning planes had suffered serious damage in combat. The flight deck crew was often pressed to the limit to keep the deck clear for incoming aircraft; often, disabled planes were simply pushed over the side.

While wounded airmen were carried off to receive medical attention in the ship's hospital, those who had returned safely gathered again in their ready room to fill out flight reports, recount their experiences, and wait for word of fellow flyers who had been picked up by American submarines, destroyers, or seaplanes.

A downed Japanese Zero leaves a flaming trail over the Palau islands (enlargement from motion-picture frame). July 1944. *Dwight Long*

Fighters and torpedo-bombers from the USS *Yorktown* fly in formation high above the Pacific clouds. October 1943. *Charles Kerlee*

Three Japanese oilers burn in Camranh Bay, off the coast of Indochina, after an attack by torpedo-bombers from the USS *Hornet*. January 1945. *Charles Kerlee*

A Curtiss SB2C Helldiver returning to the USS *Hornet* after a strike against Japanese shipping in the China Sea. January 1945. *Charles Kerlee*

Crewmen watch Navy planes return to the deck
of the USS *Lexington* after a strike against Mili.
November 1943. *Edward Steichen*

A Grumman F6F Hellcat taxies into position after landing on the USS *Lexington*. November 1943. *Victor Jorgensen*

The flight deck crew of the USS *Yorktown* secure Douglas SBD Dauntlesses that have just returned from a strike against Japanese-held islands. October 1943. *Charles Kerlee*

Ens. V. A. Prather, in charge of the USS *Lexington*'s flight deck crews, directs crewmen as they push a damaged plane out of the way. December 1943. *Victor Jorgensen*

Aboard the USS *Tulagi* off the coast of southern France, a plane handler gives the signal "Lock the tailwheel" to the pilot of a Grumman F6F Hellcat. August 1944. *Wayne Miller*

Aircrewman Alva Parker, who suffered shrapnel wounds during a raid on Rabaul, is helped from a Douglas Dauntless on the USS *Saratoga*. November 5, 1943. *Wayne Miller*

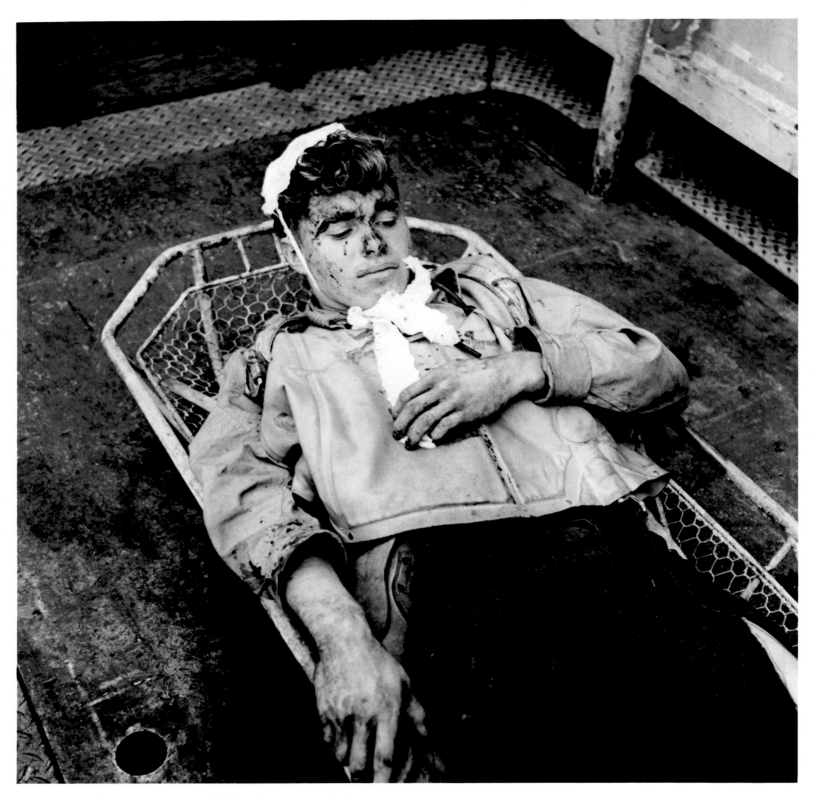

An aircrewman, wounded in the neck and shoulders during a strike against Rabaul, rests in a litter aboard the USS *Saratoga*. November 5, 1943. *Wayne Miller*

A downed Navy pilot in the South Pacific waits
in a life raft for the rescue plane. April 1944.
Horace Bristol

Wounded gunner Kenneth Bratton is lifted
from the turret of a torpedo-bomber on his return to the USS *Saratoga* from a raid on Rabaul.
By applying a tourniquet to his leg, Bratton
had remained conscious, and helped to fight off
attacking Japanese planes. November 5, 1943.
Wayne Miller

Avenger pilot Roland ("Rip") Gift (holding drink) relaxes in the USS *Monterey*'s ready room after a night landing on the carrier during the Second Battle of the Philippine Sea. June 20, 1944.
Victor Jorgensen

Pilots of the USS *Lexington* lean across the wing of a Grumman F6F Hellcat after a successful mission. En route to Tarawa, they shot down seventeen of the twenty Japanese planes they encountered. November 1943. *Edward Steichen*

In the ready room of the USS *Lexington*, an aircrewman hands in a report after a successful mission. November 1943. *Edward Steichen*

A pilot in the ready room of the USS *Yorktown* describes the divebombing mission over Wake Island. October 1943. *Charles Kerlee*

Comdr. J. C. Clifton, leader of the USS *Sara-toga*'s fighter group, passes out cigars in the carrier's ready room after a successful mission against Rabaul. November 5, 1943. *Wayne Miller*

Rear Admiral Calvin Durgin, seated with his back to the camera, joins a group of pilots in the ready room of the USS *Tulagi*. They have just completed a strike against targets beyond the range of Navy guns in southern France. August 1944. *Wayne Miller*

Enlisted personnel trading wisecracks during a
quiet moment on the USS *Lexington*. November
1943. *Victor Jorgensen*

Crewmen laughing as they listen to ships' pilots humorously describe, over the ship's bullhorn, an encounter with Japanese planes. November 1943. *Edward Steichen*

Crewmen of the USS *Lexington* listen intently as pilots describe, over the ship's loudspeaker, their attack on Kwajalein. December 1943. *Edward Steichen*

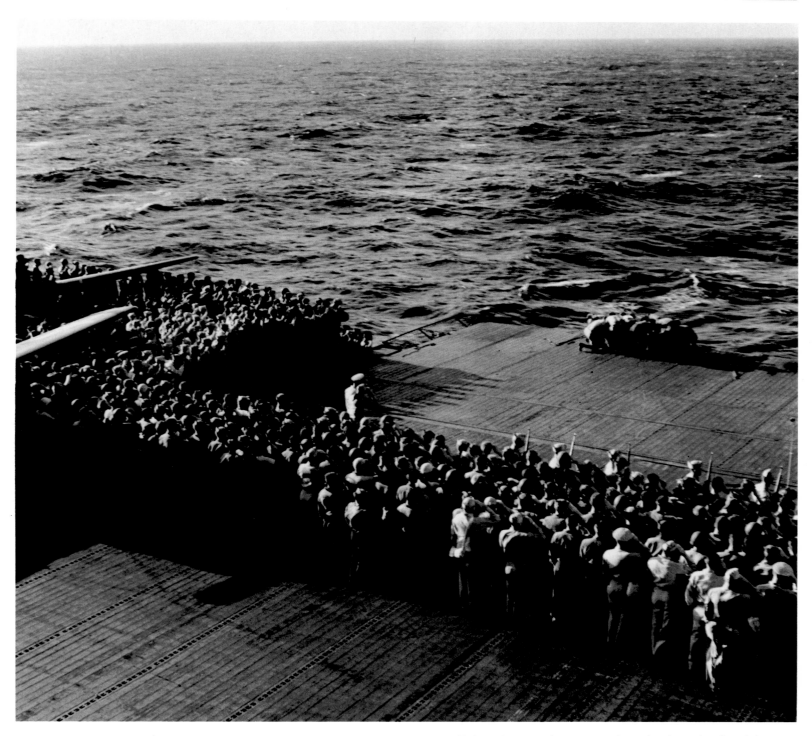

All hands stand at attention during the burial rites held for two crewmen of the USS *Lexington*. November 1943. *Victor Jorgensen*

Rest and Recreation

To its crew, a carrier might be home for the war's duration—a floating miniature city with its own doctors, dentists, organized sports, and nightly movies. Despite its size, living conditions were often cramped, and the crew took meals and showers in shifts. Pinups—demure by today's standards—were avidly collected by men who might go for a year or longer without setting eyes on a flesh-and-blood female. Once every few months, crewmen could expect to step ashore for a few hours at some remote "rest and recreation" island like Mogmog, in Ulithi atoll. Pilots, who were scheduled to rotate out of combat every six months, enjoyed greater opportunities for winning leave-time in places like Hawaii, Australia, and New Zealand.

Enlisted men relax on the flight deck of the USS *Lexington*. November 1943. *Edward Steichen*

Sunday services conducted on board the USS
Mobile, en route to attack a Japanese base on
Marcus Island. August 1943. *Alphonso Ianelli*
(Ianelli was one of the enlisted men assigned to
the Naval Aviation unit)

Admiral Lord Louis Mountbatten, commander
of Britain's Pacific fleet, addresses the crew of
the USS *Saratoga*, anchored off Ceylon. April
1944. *Wayne Miller*

Enlisted men reading on the edge of the ship's
elevator on the USS *Lexington*. November 1943.
Edward Steichen

Officers in the USS *Lexington*'s flight deck control office. December 1944. *Photographer unidentified*

Sailors of the USS *Saratoga* who had their hair clipped during a Neptune party while crossing the equator. February 1944. *Wayne Miller*

A sailor with a stack of sandwiches on the USS *Monterey*. June 1944. *Victor Jorgensen*

Aircrewmen of the USS *Ticonderoga* inspecting a pinup in the carrier's ready room. November 1944. *Wayne Miller*

Marine Pfc. Elmer McDaniel of the USS *Lexington* decorated his work jumper with what he called a "Jawja" peach. November 1943. *Edward Steichen*

One sailor inspects another sailor's tattoos aboard the USS *New Jersey*. December 1944. *Fenno Jacobs*

Enlisted men exercise on the deck of the USS
Lexington en route to the South Pacific. November 1943. *Edward Steichen*

Crewmen of the USS *Monterey* play basketball in the carrier's forward elevator. On the left, jumping for the ball, is Ens. Gerald R. Ford, future president of the United States. June 1944.
Victor Jorgensen

Having outlived their usefulness, playing cards, much-read magazines, and other articles are cast over the side of a PT boat in waters off the Philippines. December 1944. *Wayne Miller*

A landing craft loaded with men from the USS *Intrepid* heads for the recreation center on Mogmog island. April 1945. *Photographer unidentified*

Enlisted men relax on Mogmog island, lounging
about with plenty of beer. November 1944. *Fenno
Jacobs*

Navy pilots on liberty at the officers' bar on Mogmog island. February 1945. *Charles Kerlee*

Navy pilots on leave dancing with their dates in the recreation room of the Chris Holmes Rest Home in Hawaii. March 1944. *Fenno Jacobs*

A Navy pilot and his date sit under tropical vegetation at the Chris Holmes Rest Home in Hawaii. March 1944. *Fenno Jacobs*

Taking the Islands

The amphibious invasions of islands like Tarawa, Saipan, and Okinawa produced some of the most savage fighting of the war. Although relentless Naval bombardment and air strikes by carrier-based planes might begin up to a week before the actual landings, the Marines and soldiers who clambered out of their landing craft could expect to find a tenacious enemy dug in and waiting. Casualties were often high, and uncommon valor an everyday occurrence. After taking some key islands, the Navy adopted a highly successful strategy of "leapfrogging" other Japanese-held islands—cutting them off from supply and leaving them to "wither on the vine." The pace of the advance across the Pacific was thus quickened, and needless sacrifice avoided.

Once secured, many islands were quickly transformed by the Navy's Seabees into advanced bases teeming with men and supplies. Airstrips were bulldozed, roads were built, living quarters constructed, radio and telephone communications established, and fire departments and hospitals put into operation. A semblance of normal life took shape. However, for the Seabee marooned on a remote Pacific island for months on end, the unnerving sense of isolation from both the war and the United States sometimes produced a frustrating feeling of going "coral happy."

Marines move past the remains of a Japanese dive bomber on their way to Agat beach on Guam. July 1944. *Paul Dorsey*

A Douglas SBD Dauntless dive bomber over
Wake Island. October 5 or 6, 1943. *Charles Kerlee*

Japanese positions on Marcus Island go up in smoke after a raid by planes from the USS *Yorktown*. September 1943. *Charles Kerlee*

Aerial view of the invasion of Engebi island in
Eniwetok atoll. Flares (left) signal the fleet to
lift the bombardment so that landing craft
may proceed to the beaches. February 18, 1944.
Wayne Miller

Aerial view of the Marine amphibious invasion of Engebi island in Eniwetok atoll. Landing craft filled with assault troops head through a smoke screen toward the beaches. February 18, 1944. *Wayne Miller*

Marines evacuate a wounded comrade from the front lines for medical treatment on Iwo Jima. March 1945. *Paul Dorsey*

Marine Lt. Gen. Holland M. ("Howlin' Mad") Smith takes a jeep tour of a captured airfield on Saipan. July 1944. *Paul Dorsey*

Marines advance behind a tank during the battle
for Guam. July 1944. *Paul Dorsey*

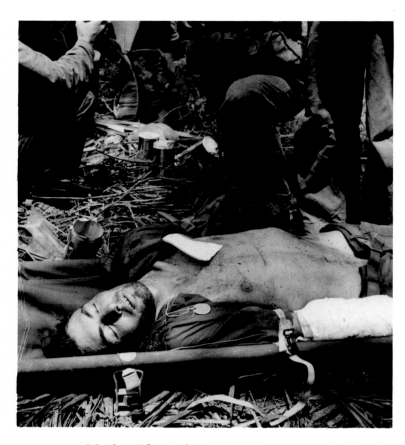

Marine Pfc. Arthur N. Robison, wounded during the fighting on Guam, receives plasma at a first-aid station. July 1944. *Paul Dorsey*

Marines, wounded in fighting on Iwo Jima, await evacuation to Guam. March 1945. *Paul Dorsey*

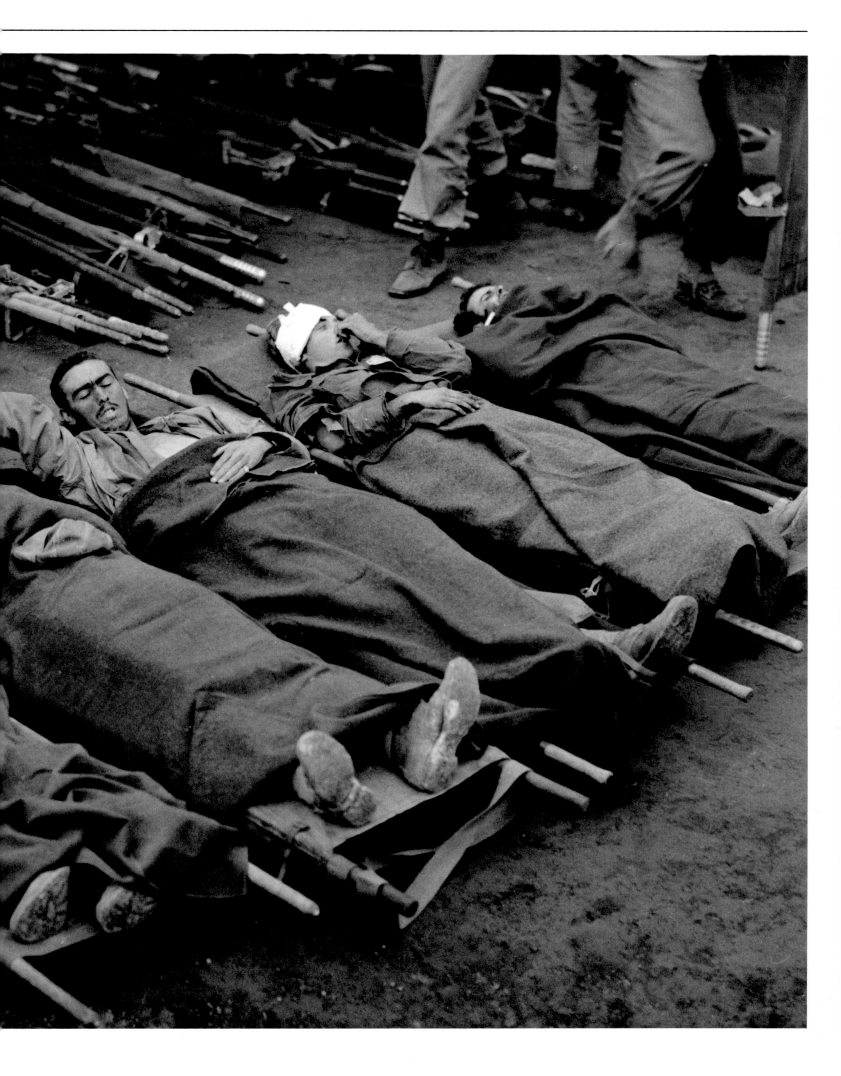

Japanese soldiers killed during the fighting on Guam. July 1944. *Paul Dorsey*

A Japanese soldier killed in a pillbox on Engebi
island. February 1944. *Wayne Miller*

A Japanese prisoner is transferred to the USS
Hornet after the plane that was evacuating him
from Saipan was shot down by Navy pilots.
June 1944. *Charles Kerlee*

Ammunition belts mark a grave at a cemetery
for American servicemen at Bougainville.
February 1944. *Fenno Jacobs*

Helmets and artillery shells serve as temporary markers on the graves of Marines who died taking Tarawa. November 1943. *Charles Kerlee*

The hand of a Japanese soldier killed in a bomb blast emerges from the rubble covering Iwo Jima. March 1945. *Edward Steichen*

A small flower, the only living thing in sight, pokes up through the debris covering a hillside on Iwo Jima. March 1945. *Edward Steichen*

Grim humor on Tarawa. November or December
1943. *Charles Kerlee*

A Japanese prisoner on Guam waits to be questioned by intelligence officers. July 1944. *Paul Dorsey*

Kwajalein Island, seen after its capture, shows
the devastating effects of Naval bombardment.
February 1944. *Charles Kerlee*

Seabees' bulldozers carve out an airstrip on
Eniwetok island. March 1944. *Charles Kerlee*

Marines installing telephone communications lines on Peleliu. In the background is part of Bloody Nose Ridge, scene of some of the fiercest fighting during the battle for the island. September 1944. *Paul Dorsey*

Aerial view of Kwajalein after the Marine invasion. The fleet in the background brought in the supplies to set up an advanced base on the island. March 1944. *Charles Kerlee*

Mechanics elevate the tail of a Chance-Vought F4U Corsair before aligning the plane's machine guns at a Marine advanced base in the South Pacific. February 1944. *Horace Bristol*

Marines walk down a line of Curtiss SB2C Hell-divers on Falalop island, Ulithi atoll. December 1944. *Thomas Binford*

A Marine pilot based on Majuro island stands on the wing of his plane. August 1944. *Paul Dorsey*

The insignia of Marine Squadron 217, based on Bougainville. February 1944. *Fenno Jacobs*

Sgt. J. S. Wilson paints a design on the prow of a bomber based at Eniwetok. June 1944. *Fenno Jacobs*

On Bougainville, Ens. Andy Jagger, a pilot of the Navy's VF-17 squadron, describes an air battle over Rabaul to Lt. H. A. March. February 1944. *Fenno Jacobs*

Marine airmen on Bougainville island relax on
the wings of their plane between strikes. April
1944. *Fenno Jacobs*

Navy personnel on Munda, New Georgia, gather around Chief Yeoman Willis to receive their mail. February 1944. *Horace Bristol*

Marines wash in hastily built showers on Namur
island. March 1944. *Charles Kerlee*

Marines swimming at Eniwetok. March 1944.
Charles Kerlee

A windmill washing machine improvised by
Marines based on Eniwetok island. June 1944.
Fenno Jacobs

A Marine on guard duty walks past a line of clothes drying on Roi island. July 1944. *Charles Kerlee*

A sign on Tarawa illustrates the Marines' estimate of the length of the war. June 1944. *Fenno Jacobs*

A tired member of the Navy's land-based VF-17 air group pauses under the squadron scoreboard on Bougainville island. February 1944. *Fenno Jacobs*

The Death of the President

Late on the afternoon of Thursday, April 12, 1945, the wire services flashed the startling news that the nation's commander-in-chief had died suddenly at his "little White House" in Warm Springs, Georgia. The next morning, a casket containing the body of the president was placed on a train to begin its journey to the nation's capital. At many stations along the route, crowds gathered on the platforms to bid a last farewell to Franklin D. Roosevelt, the man who had led the country during the past twelve years.

The train reached Union Station in Washington on Saturday morning, April 14, which had been declared a day of national mourning. The flag-draped casket was set on a black caisson drawn by six white horses. In traditional fashion, a seventh horse, the commander-in-chief's own mount, walked alone, its stirrups reversed. The procession moved slowly past the solemn crowd that lined Constitution and Pennsylvania avenues, the stillness punctuated only by the beat of muffled drums. After a short ceremony at the White House, a large funeral party continued on by train to the Roosevelt estate at Hyde Park, New York. There, on Sunday morning, a bugler blew final taps as the casket was lowered into the earth in the family rose garden.

A street scene in Washington, D.C., following the announcement of FDR's death. The headline inside the newspaper reads, "Stalin mourns F.D.R." April 13, 1945. *Wayne Miller*

The headline of the Washington *Evening Star* announces a national day of mourning after President Franklin D. Roosevelt's death. April 13, 1945. *Wayne Miller*

Men in Washington, D.C., reading newspaper
accounts the morning after FDR's death. April
14, 1945. *Wayne Miller*

Two women stop before a portrait of Roosevelt, surrounded by lilies, in a shopwindow in Washington, D.C. April 12 or 13, 1945. *Wayne Miller*

A man gazes into a shopwindow shortly after
the announcement of FDR's death. April 12 or
13, 1945. *Wayne Miller*

A crowd gathered in front of the White House awaits further news after the announcement of FDR's death. April 12, 1945. *Fenno Jacobs*

Franklin D. Roosevelt's flag-draped casket, placed on an artillery caisson, is accompanied by a military honor guard as the funeral procession sets out from Union Station on its way to the White House. April 14, 1945. *Photographer unidentified*

The faces of some of the thousands of mourners who lined the streets of the nation's capital as the funeral cortege of President Franklin D. Roosevelt passed by. April 14, 1945. *Wayne Miller*

Faces along the route of FDR's funeral cortege. April 14, 1945. *Wayne Miller*

Faces along the route of FDR's funeral cortege.
April 14, 1945. *Wayne Miller*

Stunned public reaction in Washington, D.C., after the announcement of FDR's death. April 12, 1945. *Fenno Jacobs*

The burial of President Franklin D. Roosevelt
on the grounds of the family estate at Hyde
Park, New York. April 15, 1945. *Wayne Miller*

The Last Days

Victory in the European war in May 1945 enabled the United States to turn all of its resources to the war against Japan. By this time the Navy controlled the waters around the Japanese home islands; flying from bases in the Marianas, the Army's B-29 bombers had begun to unleash fire-storms which swept through Tokyo. But off Okinawa, the Japanese staged a last-ditch effort at retaliation, and the suicide tactics of the kamikaze pilots proved alarmingly effective against American warships. Worse was expected to be in store for the projected Allied landings on the Japanese mainland in the fall of 1945.

It never proved necessary, for on August 6, a single American bomber exploded an atomic device in the air over Hiroshima, a city with 344,000 inhabitants on the southern tip of Japan's main island. Four square miles of the city vanished; 80,000 people were killed and thousands more left to die slowly of radiation poisoning. Three days later, a second atomic bomb was dropped on Nagasaki, with equally devastating results. On August 14, the Japanese surrender was announced, setting off two days of wild celebration in the United States. By the end of August, American troops began to occupy Tokyo, and on September 2, the formal surrender ceremony took place on the battleship USS *Missouri* in Tokyo Bay. Shortly afterward, the bombed cities were opened to correspondents, who were able to see for the first time the awesome human cost of atomic warfare.

Sailors who were wounded in battle catch up on American newspapers after reaching San Francisco on the USS *President Hayes*. January 1945. *Paul Dorsey*

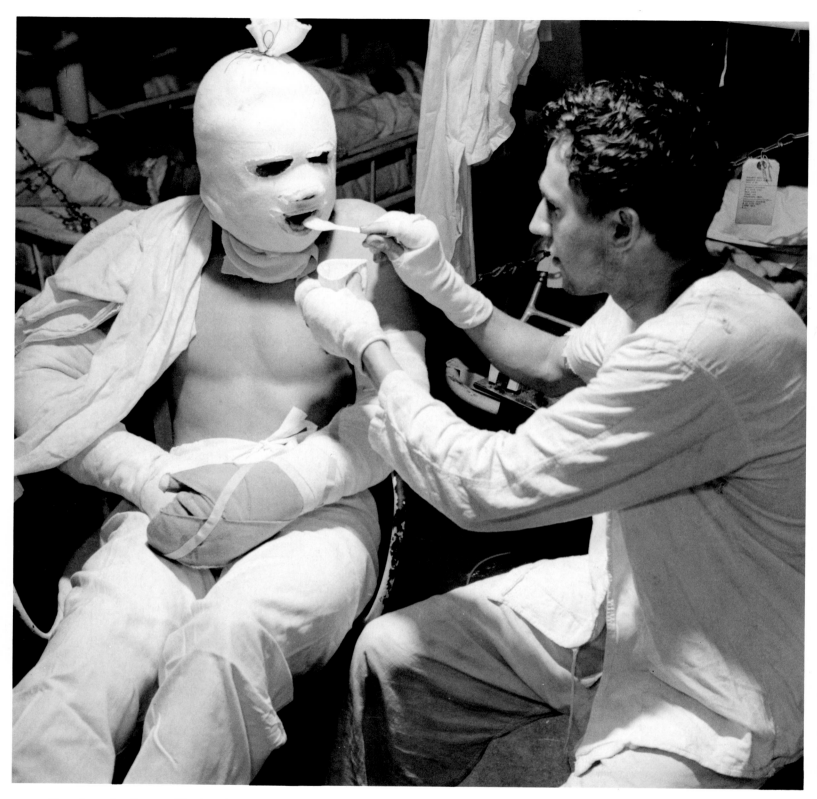

Bandaged after suffering burns when his ship
was hit by a kamikaze, a sailor is fed aboard the
hospital ship USS *Solace*. May 1945. *Victor
Jorgensen*

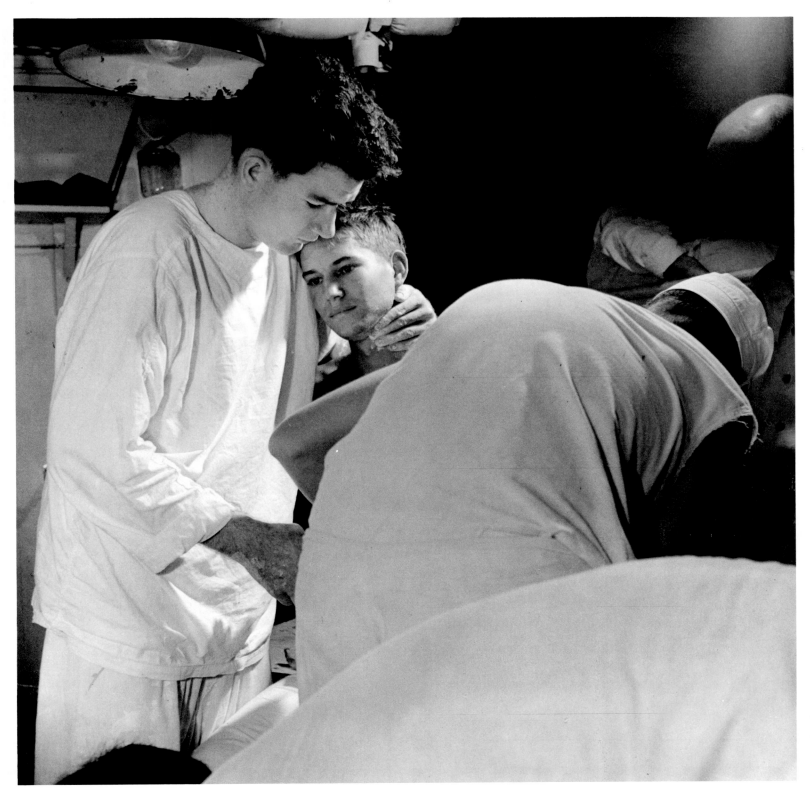

Pvt. J. B. Slagle receives his daily dressing of wounds on board the USS *Solace* en route from Okinawa to Guam. May 1945. *Victor Jorgensen*

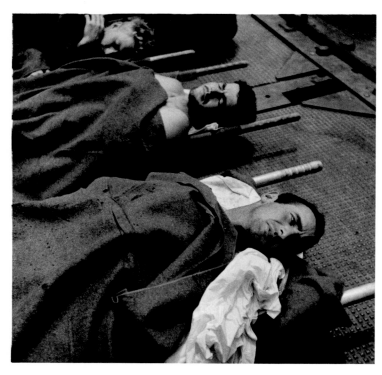

Men wounded on Okinawa are lined up on a pontoon dock, waiting for transfer to a hospital ship anchored offshore. May 1945. *Victor Jorgensen*

Japanese soldiers who surrendered at Kerama-retto during the Okinawa campaign on a U.S. carrier. May 1945. *Thomas Binford*

Japanese soldiers wade through the water to surrender to the crew of a Navy picket boat on Kerama-retto during the Okinawa campaign. May 1945. *Thomas Binford*

Japanese prisoners of war are led off a submarine at a base in the Pacific. May 1945. *Horace
Bristol*

The crewmen of the battleship USS *New Jersey* watch a Japanese prisoner of war bathe himself before he is issued GI clothing. November 1944. *Fenno Jacobs*

Devastated downtown Manila. In the foreground sits a *calesa*, a two-wheeled taxi pulled by its driver. May 1945. *Victor Jorgensen*

A sailor on liberty at a fruit stand in Manila.
May 1945. *Victor Jorgensen*

Filipino children and Naval officers in downtown Manila. May 1945. *Victor Jorgensen*

Filipinos in *bancas* paddle out to anchored destroyers to trade with the crew. June 1945.
Victor Jorgensen

New Yorkers celebrate the Japanese surrender.
August 15, 1945. *Victor Jorgensen*

Operation Snapshot: the Fast-carrier Task Force of Admiral Halsey's Third Fleet maneuvers off the coast of Japan. August 16 or 17, 1945. *Barrett Gallagher*

Another view of Operation Snapshot.

Japanese envoys, led by General Yoshijuro Umezu, Chief of the Imperial General Staff, leave the USS *Missouri* in Tokyo Bay after signing the surrender papers. September 2, 1945.
Barrett Gallagher

A sailor rides a Japanese bicycle through the streets of Tokyo. September 1945. *Wayne Miller*

Marine Cpl. L. A. Mulikowski sits on a hospital bed on board the USS *Benevolence* after being freed from a prison camp where he had been held for three years. August 1945. *Wayne Miller*

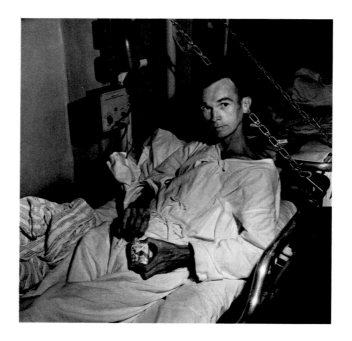

Japanese civil police watch as Allied prisoners leave a Franciscan convent in Saitama prefecture, north of Tokyo, used as a prison during the war. August 1945. *Wayne Miller*

Scores of Allied prisoners at a prison in Saitama prefecture, north of Tokyo, cheer the arrival of Navy and Marine personnel. August 1945. *Wayne Miller*

Demobilized Japanese soldiers waiting to board
trains that will return them to their homes.
September 1945. *Wayne Miller*

Demobilized Japanese soldiers crowd trains that will return them to their homes. September 1945. *Wayne Miller*

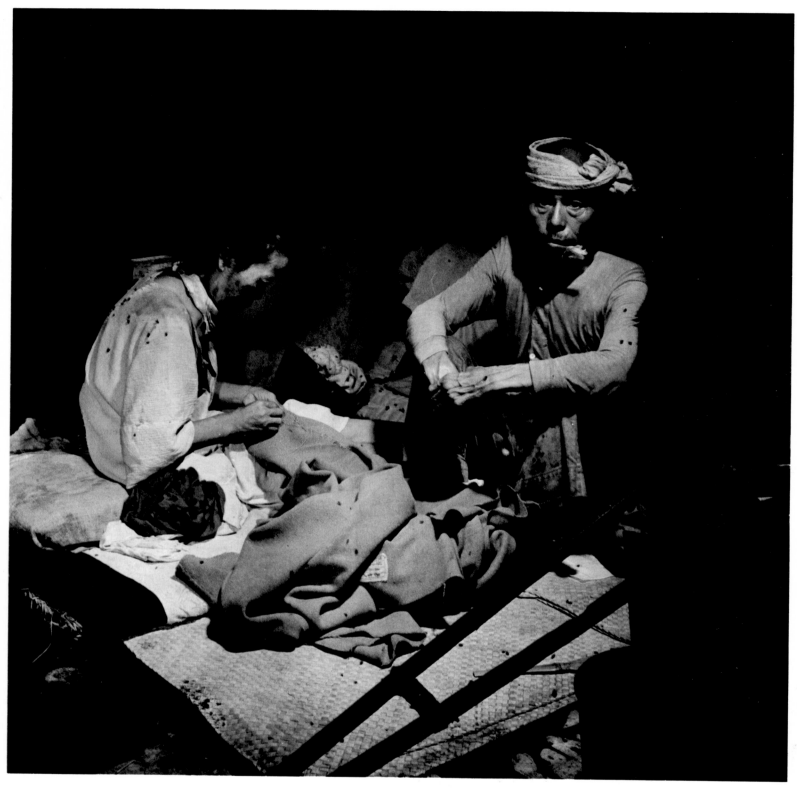

Victims of the Hiroshima blast in a fly-infested makeshift hospital in a bank building. September 1945. *Wayne Miller*

A Japanese soldier walks through a leveled area near the blast center in Hiroshima. September 1945. *Wayne Miller*

A victim of the atomic blast at Hiroshima lies in
a makeshift hospital in a bank building. September 1945. *Wayne Miller*

The neat packages stacked in this Buddhist temple are ceremonial boxes containing the ashes of cremated victims of the Hiroshima blast. September 1945. *Wayne Miller*

Demobilized Japanese soldiers at the end of
World War II. September 1945. *Wayne Miller*

Acknowledgments

My interest in Edward Steichen's photographic activities in the U.S. Navy dates from the spring of 1979, when I had the good fortune to work with Marianne Fulton, Curator of 20th Century Photography at the George Eastman House, in preparing a tribute to Steichen and his work on the centennial of his birth. My biographical research preliminary to the exhibition led me to believe that Steichen's Navy years might reward further exploration. Initial encouragement came from Ms. Fulton and Robert Doherty, then director of the George Eastman House.

In 1979–80 I completed a master's thesis on the subject for the Rochester Institute of Technology; I am grateful for the advice and assistance of Professors Charles Arnold, Jr., and Elliot Rubenstein, and for the warm support of Dr. Richard Zakia.

A special debt is owed to Grace M. Mayer, Curator Emeritus of the Department of Photography of the Museum of Modern Art, for her continuing encouragement, and for her generosity in allowing me repeated access to material in that museum's Edward Steichen Archive.

The story of the Naval Aviation unit could not have been told without the assistance of the photographers themselves. My thanks to Horace Bristol, Barrett Gallagher, Charles Kerlee, Victor Jorgensen, and Wayne Miller for sharing their experiences. Thanks also to Marty Forscher for providing details of the operation of the unit's photographic laboratory.

For their willingness to provide insights and information, in correspondence and conversation, I am grateful to Ansel Adams, Mrs. Helga Sandburg Crile, Oliver Jensen, George Kidder Smith, David H. McAlpin, Thomas J. Maloney, John Archer Morton, Edwin Rosskam, Arthur Rothstein, and Miss Kate Steichen.

The staff of the Still Picture Branch, U.S. National Archives, was unfailingly helpful during my picture research, and provided the excellent prints that are reproduced in this book.

I wish also to express my thanks for the diverse services rendered by Mikki Carpenter, Department of Rights and Reproductions, Museum of Modern Art; Keith Davis, Curator, Hallmark Photographic Collection; Diana Edkins, Condé Nast Publications; Andrew Eskind, Assistant Director, George Eastman House; Ann Fallen, Staples and Charles, Washington, D.C.; Charles Haberlein, Jr., Naval Historical Center Photographic Section, Washington, D.C.; Jon Holmes; Susan Kramarsky, George Eastman House; A. T. Wooldridge, Associate Curator of Aeronautics, Air and Space Museum, Smithsonian Institution; and Christopher Zimmerman, WXXI-TV, Rochester, N.Y.

Finally, heartfelt thanks to my wife, Talbot Malcolm, for gracefully enduring a clattering typewriter at odd hours.

Bibliography

Hurley, F. Jack. *Portrait of a Decade: Roy Stryker and the Development of Documentary Photography in the Thirties* (Baton Rouge: Louisiana State University Press, 1972; reprinted in 1977 by DaCapo Press, New York).

Jensen, Oliver. *Carrier War* (New York: Simon and Schuster, 1945).

Josephson, Matthew. "Commander with a Camera." *The New Yorker*, June 3, 1944, pp. 26–32; and June 10, 1944, pp. 27–37.

Morison, Samuel Eliot. *The Two-Ocean War: A Short History of the United States Navy in the Second World War* (Boston/Toronto: Atlantic Monthly Press/Little, Brown and Company, 1945).

Reynolds, Clark G. *The Fast Carriers: The Forging of an Air Navy* (New York: McGraw-Hill Book Company, 1968).

Sandburg, Carl. *Home Front Memo* (New York: Harcourt, Brace and Company, 1943).

———. *Steichen the Photographer* (New York: Harcourt, Brace and Company, 1929).

Steichen, Edward. *The Blue Ghost: A Photographic Log and Personal Narrative of the Aircraft Carrier USS Lexington in Combat Operations* (New York: Harcourt, Brace and Company, 1947).

———. *A Life in Photography* (New York: Doubleday and Company, 1963).

———, ed. *Power in the Pacific* (New York: US Camera Publishing Company, 1945).

———, ed. *U.S. Navy War Photographs* (New York: US Camera Publishing Company, 1946).

Stott, William. *Documentary Expression and Thirties America* (New York: Oxford University Press, 1973).

Index

All references are to page numbers; illustrations are indicated by *italic numerals*.

The photographs of the Naval Aviation Photographic Unit were reproduced from negatives in the collection of the National Archives. The National Archive negative identification numbers are given page by page:

Title page: 80-G-324556; copyright page: 80-G-417667; p. 12: 18-E-6233A; p. 21: 80-G-474615; p. 23: 80-G-468286; p. 24 (above): 80-G-43860; (below): 80-G-468273; p. 25: 80-G-468290; p. 26 (above): 80-G-468266; (below): 80-G-468297; p. 30: 80-G-361481; p. 31: 80-G-472661; p. 34 (above): 80-G-475616; (below): 80-G-475436; p. 35: 80-G-475409; p. 37: 80-G-468269; p. 39: 80-G-415001; p. 41: 80-G-468291; p. 42 (above): 80-G-305229; (below): 80-G-474135; p. 43: 80-G-474152; p. 47: 80-G-475013; p. 48: 80-G-474310; p. 49: 80-G-412471; p. 58: 80-G-412756; p. 59: 80-G-412719; p. 60 (above): 80-G-412735; (below): 80-G-412723; p. 61: 80-G-412634; p. 62: 80-G-475960; p. 63: 80-G-475984; p. 64 (above): 80-G-475999; (below): 80-G-412639; p. 65: 80-G-475980; p. 66: 80-G-412683; p. 67: 80-G-412633; p. 68: 80-G-412712; p. 73: 80-G-377208; p. 74 (above): 80-G-473446; (below): 80-G-441160; p. 75: 80-G-405375; p. 76: 80-G-472375; p. 77: 80-G-469839; p. 78: 80-G-469691; p. 79: 80-G-474788; p. 80 (above): 80-G-470021; (below): 80-G-469688; p. 81: 80-G-43089; p. 84: 80-G-225251; p. 86: 80-G-470228; p. 87: 80-G-473512; p. 88: 80-G-468128; p. 89 (above): 80-G-335390; (below): 80-G-468169; p. 90 (above): 80-G-469994; (below): 80-G-469992; p. 91: 80-G-469993; p. 92 (above): 80-G-47015; (below): 80-G-469929; p. 93: 80-G-469976; p. 94 (above): 80-G-470859; (below): 80-G-431055; p. 95: 80-G-469289; p. 96: 80-G-476250; p. 97: 80-G-474168; p. 98: 80-G-470269; p. 99: 80-G-342482; p. 100 (above): 80-G-471182; (below): 80-G-471240; p. 101: 80-G-468912; p. 105: 80-G-431063; p. 106: 80-G-468977; p. 107: 80-G-470943; p. 108: 80-G-431069; p. 109: 80-G-470183; p. 110: 80-G-41869; p. 111: 80-G-415478; p. 112: 80-G-414667; p. 113: 80-G-470922; p. 114: 80-G-471214; p. 115: 80-G-469383; p. 116: 80-G-470673; p. 117: 80-G-468756; p. 118: 80-G-432851; p. 119: 80-G-471189; p. 120 (above): 80-G-471179; (below): 80-G-418194; p. 121: 80-G-415580; p. 124: 80-G-474444; p. 125: 80-G-476108; p. 126: 80-G-469317; p. 127: 80-G-320999; p. 128: 80-G-471242; p. 129: 80-G-471196; p. 130: 80-G-473547; p. 131: 80-G-417636; p. 132: 80-G-468782; p. 133: 80-G-470918; p. 134: 80-G-470905; p. 135: 80-G-474000; p. 136: 80-G-415477; p. 137: 80-G-474791; p. 139: 80-G-470985; p. 140: 80-G-471311; p. 141: 80-G-432598; p. 142: 80-G-417635; p. 143: 80-G-305235; p. 144: 80-G-471210; p. 145: 80-G-470987; p. 146: 80-G-471283; p. 147: 80-G-473084; p. 150: 80-G-471232; p. 152: 80-G-470528; p. 153: 80-G-470720; p. 154: 80-G-470981; p. 155: 80-G-471782; p. 156 (above): 80-G-470778; (below): 80-G-468794; p. 157: 80-G-469511; p. 158: 80-G-470178; p. 159: 80-G-470222; p. 160: 80-G-470188; p. 161: 80-G-417628; p. 162: 80-G-472497; p. 163: 80-G-412962; p. 164: 80-G-408188; p. 165: 80-G-408126; p. 166: 80-G-475095; p. 167: 80-G-475096; p. 171: 80-G-475146; p. 172: 80-G-43454; p. 173: 80-G-474367; p. 174: 80-G-470712; p. 175: 80-G-216213; p. 176 (above): 80-G-412493; (below): 80-G-475157; p. 177: 80-G-475150; p. 178: 80-G-474792; p. 179: 80-G-476381; p. 180: 80-G-475147; p. 182: 80-G-401064; p. 183: 80-G-469307; p. 184: 80-G-476284; p. 185: 80-G-401598; p. 186: 80-G-412532; p. 187: 80-G-412461; p. 188: 80-G-476259; p. 189: 80-G-475166; p. 190: 80-G-400960; p. 191: 80-G-401665; p. 192: 80-G-408157; p. 193: 80-G-400949; p. 194: 80-G-450046; p. 195: 80-G-408109; p. 197: 80-G-401047; p. 198 (above): 80-G-476287; (below): 80-G-401702; p. 199: 80-G-475024; p. 200: 80-G-472195; p. 201: 80-G-471407; p. 202: 80-G-401090; p. 203: 80-G-401169; p. 204: 80-G-401720; p. 205: 80-G-401089; p. 206: 80-G-476304; p. 207: 80-G-475093; p. 210: 80-G-377535; p. 211: 80-G-377529; p. 212: 80-G-377545; p. 213: 80-G-377530; p. 214: 80-G-377532; p. 215: 80-G-377605; p. 216: 80-G-315485; p. 217 (above): 80-G-377562; (below): 80-G-377554; p. 218: 80-G-377572; p. 219: 80-G-377588; p. 220–21: 80-G-377584; p. 225: 80-G-377613; p. 226: 80-G-346694; p. 227: 80-G-413963; p. 228: 80-G-472355; p. 229: 80-G-474957; p. 231: 80-G-474954; p. 232: 80-G-468228; p. 233: 80-G-469956; p. 234: 80-G-474859; p. 235: 80-G-474870; p. 236: 80-G-474809; p. 237: 80-G-474852; p. 238: 80-G-377099; p. 239 (above): 80-G-472620; (below): 80-G-490362; p. 241: 80-G-415309; p. 242: 80-G-472629; p. 243: 80-G-473728; p. 244 (above): 80-G-473727; (below): 80-G-473711; p. 245: 80-G-473730; p. 246: 80-G-473751; p. 247: 80-G-473743; p. 248: 80-G-473741; p. 249: 80-G-473733; p. 250: 80-G-473739; p. 251: 80-G-473753; p. 252: 80-G-473755.